Intellectual Capital

Intellectual Capital

The Intangible Assets of
Professional Development Schools

Edited by
Carole G. Basile

Published by
State University of New York Press, Albany

For information, contact State University of New York Press, Albany, NY
www.sunypress.edu

Production by Kelli W. LeRoux
Marketing by Michael Campochiaro

Library of Congress Cataloging-in-Publication Data

Intellectual capital : the intangible assets of professional development
schools / [edited by] Carole Basile.
   p. cm.
Includes bibliographical references and index.
ISBN 978-1-4384-2661-7 (hardcover : alk. paper)
   1. Laboratory schools—United States. 2. College-school cooperation—
United States. 3. Intellectual capital—United States. I. Basile, Carole G.,
1958–
LB2154.A3I58 2009
370.71'1—dc22   2009017038

10 9 8 7 6 5 4 3 2 1

Thank you to all of our partners, past and present, who have been instrumental in creating a successful teacher education program that has extended institutional boundaries and created high quality teachers for all students.

To our children and our children's children: May they always have teachers who inspire and motivate them to enjoy learning and take advantage of life's possibilities.

Contents

Foreword

Carole Basile and her colleagues have done a rare and wonderful thing in this book. They have managed to write about a topic that matters—professional development schools (PDSs)—in ways that add value due to both strong intellectual framing and specific practical applications. That they have done this in a coauthored book, as a joint team of scholars and practitioners, makes the book even more special and more useful, I think, for a variety of audiences.

The topic is important because PDSs represent the best opportunity to simultaneously improve both schools and teacher education programs. PDS partnerships have swept the nation in the 20 years since the Holmes Group envisioned them, with thousands of partnerships in place and virtually all teacher education institutions at some stage of establishing or thinking about forming them. And, while there have been dozens of books and hundreds of articles and conference presentations written or presented about PDS, most tell the "creation stories" about the formation of the PDS partnerships and focus on their synergy and "win-win" potential. As one who has reviewed this literature periodically for over a decade, I have only been able to cite a relatively few studies that report compellingly about PDS impacts; fewer still take a close look at what is inside the "black box" of PDS partnerships that contribute to their outcomes.

Basile and her colleagues help fill in this gap and do it quite elegantly. Using intellectual capital and knowledge management frameworks borrowed from business and other sectors, these scholar-practitioners tell us the inside story of PDS challenges and successes in a way that both explains the successes of PDSs and serves as a tool for improving them.

The intellectual and practical framework for this work is powerfully laid out in the first few pages of Chapter 1. If intellectual capital in the business world can be broken up as external capital (stock markets, suppliers, customers), internal capital (organizational structures and processes), and human capital (what employees know), what are the parallels in the educational sector? Basile starts by outlining the equivalents for a school (e.g., external capital would be the school district, greater community, parents, local businesses, and external organizations, including universities). She and her colleagues then go beyond applying this to an *individual* organization (like a school or a university) to use it to understand and analyze what happens to the *partnership* they create when they form a PDS. In a PDS, each partner is part of the external capital of the other, and the three forms of intellectual capital reside *within* each partner and *between* them. This means that, using the example of internal capital, there are organizational structures and processes for management within the school, separate ones within the university, as well as a third form of internal capital embedded in the PDS: the crossover processes that enable the partnership to operate.

The ability to analyze forms of tangible and intangible intellectual capital for the school, the university, and the partnership sets the stage for what, in Chapter 2, becomes a crash course in the skill of knowledge management to help maximize impacts. The "monitor" device the authors introduce provides a practical way to track the intangible assets of a PDS and serves as a wonderful complement to more traditional state accountability report cards. Chapter 3 serves to engage school leaders in the PDS process, a critical component for change.

The balance of the book provides numerous fine-grained examples that elucidate the theoretical framework and provide specific practical suggestions as well, like the four different approaches to increasing external capital in Chapter 4 or the development of distributed leadership, knowledge-sharing systems, and other forms of internal capital in Chapter 5. The stories that underlie the development of human capital in Chapter 6 and the drilling down into culture and change in Chapter 7 continue this dual function. Moreover, the book, the monitor, and the lessons learned summarized in Chapter 8 encourage us to keep our eyes on the interconnections between and among the forms of intellectual capital—how increasing external capacity can increase internal, how changes in the university's internal or human capital will affect the school, and overall, how to use the framework for learning and understanding across the school–university divide.

As someone who has argued for years that PDSs need to clearly demonstrate impacts on student learning and who devoted the largest portion of my *Professional Development School Handbook* to understanding and exploring how that happens and can be documented, I appreciate the practical contribution of this book. The intellectual framing of the book is all the more powerful because it is so clearly tied to practice;

the specific examples of real partnerships working at understanding and managing intellectual capital processes and intentionally connecting them to student outcomes are immensely valuable. They help those inside PDSs to assess where they are and tune them up to better target student learning. They also make it easier for those stakeholders outside PDSs to understand that they can and should pay attention to a range of measures beyond test scores.

Finally, this is a book that not only is of value to its readers but clearly has been of value to its many coauthors. In a world where fragmenting pressures quickly and easily pull us out of alignment, writing to a conceptual framework like this one helps people make sense of what they are doing. The authors here know they are not just laying stones but building a cathedral—developing their partnerships' capacity to improve student learning and teacher professional development. The framework not only helps us as readers but clearly has helped the author-practitioners keep their eyes on the prize of student learning, and develop some powerful tools to pursue that with intentionality and purpose.

Lee Teitel
Director
Executive Leadership Program for Educators
Harvard University

Chapter 1

Intellectual Capital and Professional Development Schools

Carole Basile

Primarily in business, but in other fields such as psychology and sociology, *intellectual capital* is what everyone knows and brings to an organization that enhances its value to others (Stewart, 1999). Researchers in the area of intellectual capital claim that assessing and managing intellectual capital is suitable for application in many different markets and in many different fields and that it creates a significant contribution to the value of the organization (Roos & Roos, 1997). The study of the organization occurs through examining both tangible and intangible assets. For example, a business has a financial statement that says one thing about the value of a company to shareholders or owners, but it also has other assets, intangible assets, that say something different about the company (i.e., numbers of clients, longevity of clients, information management systems, project management systems, employee training). When applied to the field of education, schools have accountability reports and test scores that say one thing about who they are and the school's value to students, but there are also intangible assets that should not be overlooked that are also a value to students (i.e., parent involvement, external partnerships, accountability systems, curricular frameworks, professional learning for teachers).

Although there are variations in the conceptual framework that defines intellectual capital in the business community, intellectual capital is typically comprised of three components: external capital (i.e., the stock market, the customers, the suppliers), internal capital (i.e., organizational structures, processes, management), and human capital (the knowledge, learning, and growth of employees) (Kaplan & Norton, 1996; Stewart, 1999; Sveiby, 2001).

1

Applied to education, external capital includes the school district, the greater school community, parents, local businesses, and external organizations that have a role in the school, such as a local university. Internal capital includes governance structures; curriculum development; management processes; hiring, recruiting, and retaining teachers and administrators procedures; and renewal or reform processes. Finally, human capital includes the educators' knowledge and the structures and processes for professional development.

Assessing and managing intellectual capital is critical to any organization, and in schools where intellectual capital is the keystone of the realm, it should result in students who can learn, in environments that meet their needs, and in an understanding of what educators can bring to each and every person in the community. In professional development schools (PDSs), managing intellectual capital is even more imperative, as there are more resources, systems, and knowledge to manage. If managed intentionally and properly, this university–school partnership could add value to and ultimately increase student learning.

Professional Development Schools

Professional development schools are special schools where there are unique university–school relationships that can change a school culture and add value to students and the community. Teitel (2003) stated that the biggest and, ultimately, most important questions asked in any research on PDSs concern impacts—impacts that produce improved student learning outcomes; improved preparation of preservice teachers, administrators, and other educators; and improved, continuing professional development and learning for all school- and university-based adults who work in the partnership (p. 11). The complexity of assessing a PDSs impact on student learning is well documented (Abdul-Haaq, 1998; Murrell, 1998; Teitel, 2003). The variables are numerous and difficult to isolate but include the impact of other school initiatives, the time teacher candidates spend in a particular school or classroom, the quality of teachers in the school, the leadership of the administrators, and external pressures of accountability. In addition to school variables, there are university variables, such as how the university defines a PDS, the time professors are engaged in the school, and the quality of the resources they bring to the school.

The National Council for Accreditation of Teacher Education (NCATE, 2003) provided evidence from a number of sources that PDS candidates perform better than traditionally prepared candidates (Gill & Hove,

1999; Houston, 1999; Neubert & Binko, 1998; Shroyer, Wright, & Ramey-Gassert, 1996). It is also cited that the retention of PDS-trained new teachers is three times that of traditionally prepared teachers. Also importantly, student achievement in PDSs exceeds expectations, and students in PDSs show higher gain scores when compared to non-PDSs (Gill & Hove, 1999; Pine, 2000).

However, there are still questions about what happens in a PDS, what's making a difference, what the activities look like, and what the intangible assets are that could improve student learning. Tangible assets might include reduced student–adult ratios, professional development for clinical teachers, additional leadership within the school, additional adults in the school to lead enrichment activities, and changing systems that are inclusive of new resources. Intangible assets are difficult to see and difficult to assess, but they include such things as the impact of the professional development, the extent of the relationships that build over time, changes in leadership, and the increase in student effort. Taking stock of these intangible assets that contribute to the school's intellectual capital is imperative if we are to better understand what happens in a PDS and why these assets are so important to the success of the teacher candidate and the students in the school.

Intellectual Capital, Professional Development Schools, and the Logic Model

If educators at universities and in schools are going to renew schools to close the achievement gap, they must keep their eye on the prize—student learning. In PDSs, being intentional about the wise use of resources in schools and how they complement district and school resources to build intellectual capital benefits not only the school but the school district.

The question raised by Teitel about research on PDSs remains. How do we connect the activities of the PDS partnership to student learning? Killion (2002) suggested that staff developers use a logic model to evaluate the impact of professional development on student learning. The model is a flow chart that sequences the critical components of a program, including inputs or resources, activities or processes, initial outcomes, intermediate outcomes, and results. An example might be a school district that provides instructional coaches to schools. Those coaches have activities and processes that they use to change or modify the instructional practices of teachers. It is anticipated that those changes in practice create changes in student behavior or effort and in turn increase student learning.

A PDS example might be the use of teacher candidates. Teacher candidates are a critical component that would be included in a logic model. The teacher candidate (resource) coteaches (activity) with a clinical teacher. This adds to the knowledge of both the novice and the experienced teacher (initial outcome). This causes better instruction for students (intermediate outcome) and eventually increased student learning (result). By assessing intellectual capital throughout the school and examining where the school and university meet, a school can begin to see where the logic model leads and the impact that being a PDS has on student learning.

In a PDS, the partnership between the university and the school should enhance all of the elements (external, internal, and human capital) if the partnership is sound and is fully functioning, based on the needs of an individual school. A friend of mine was once asked, "If there was one thing that could change of all of education, what would it be?" Her response was, "Get rid of all the people who believe there is just one thing that would change all of education." It's not one thing that will change all of education and increase student learning but the activities of partnerships that create motion and synergy. Partnerships, such as PDSs, can make a difference in the school and be an example of how to prepare teachers, increase teacher quality, renew curriculum, institute systems for performance, and focus on student learning at the same time.

Figure 1.1 illustrates how the models of intellectual capital and logic are combined to provide a conceptualization of how partnership activities can, through a sequence of events, increase student learning. In other words, the more you know and intentionally manage the activities of the partnership, the more likely you are to act as pistons, driving energy to the elements of intellectual capital. The more you build intellectual capital, the more you increase growth and competence and create cultural change. And finally, the more teachers, administrators, parents, and others in the community become more competent, grow, and change, the more likely it is that student learning will also be impacted in a positive direction.

The model is not one-directional, however; as the school community learns more about how students learn and how the culture responds to change and innovation and as each of the three different types of capital are increased, the activities of the partnership are informed. It is this feedback loop that implies continuous learning for everyone or simultaneous renewal.

Important to note is the concept that the partnership is the school and should be thought of as an integral part of the school. The partnership is not another program that is "extra" or "on top of" the work of the school. The school needs to think of itself as a PDS just like schools think

FIGURE 1.1. Intellectual Capital in the Professional Development School

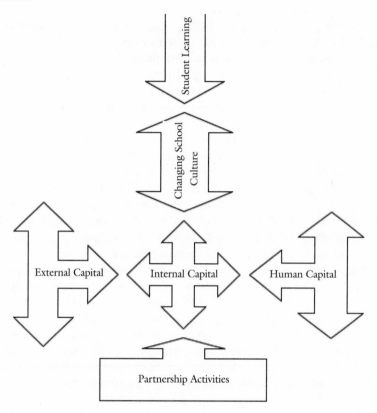

of themselves as a charter school, International Baccalaureate (IB) school, dual language school, alternative school, and so on. It's who they are, and the resources extend the possibilities of what they can do for students. This doesn't mean that they aren't something else, too—some of our PDSs are also IB schools, dual language schools, or work as professional learning communities, but it's the blending of the work that the school can utilize to boost renewal efforts.

In 1993, the teacher education program at the University of Colorado Denver (UCD) was redesigned, moving from traditional student-teaching placements across the metro area to fully integrated courses and field work conducted in partnership with PDSs. The program had as its theme "Teacher Leaders for Tomorrow's Schools," building on the deep experiences that most of the teacher candidates brought to this teacher education program. Since that time, the teacher education program has become a model of instructional and learning excellence within a PDS design.

We currently partner with 23 PDS sites across six Denver metropolitan school districts that primarily serve students from low-income and ethnically diverse backgrounds: Adams Five Star School District, Adams County 14, Denver Public Schools, Douglas County Schools, Aurora Public Schools, and Jefferson County Schools. Our partnership program reflects an urban mission to ensure that new teachers are skilled in working with diverse populations. We prepare approximately 400 teacher candidates each year at the graduate, postbaccalaureate, and undergraduate levels.

Preservice teachers spend approximately 100 days, 8 hours per day, of the school year in a single PDS at the elementary level and across a middle and high school PDS at the secondary level. Each PDS has the support of a university site professor (a faculty member who works at the school 1 day per week for the length of the school year) and the school's site coordinator (a master teacher on special assignment and released from normal teaching duties). The site professor and site coordinator work together as a team to prepare 12–15 teacher candidates each year, to provide professional development for classroom teachers, to engage in the reform of curriculum and instruction, and to conduct research or inquiry, all with a focus on the improvement of student learning.

Throughout this book, we hope to provide the reader with evidence that being a PDS can impact student learning. As a business is not solely measured by its financial statement, a PDS can not simply be measured by its test scores. Intangible assets are important to the value the PDS has for all students and the significance of the partnership.

Chapter 2 presents an "intangible asset monitor" that we have adapted for our PDS environment that gives schools a tool for continuous monitoring of the partnership activities. Using this monitor can ensure that the activities and systems match school goals and resources are being utilized wisely. The monitor is also a planning tool. It can provide school leadership teams with ways of thinking about the partnership that will promote the partnership within the community for sustainability, create systems that utilize the partnership resources for meeting school goals, and find opportunities to continue professional learning and increasing instructional quality.

Subsequent chapters provide in-depth essays from PDSs that exemplify how intellectual capital is changing the culture of each school and the benefits to student learning. Each story has been written by those that have been closest to the school, the site professors, site coordinators, teachers, and others. They are told in their words and from their perspectives. Each essay briefly describes the school or context in which the work is being done, describes the project or activities and the link to intellectual capital, and provides commentary about the impacts the work is having on its stakeholders.

These stories are important to us, and we believe that they will be important for others who are also using a PDS model and for those considering it. Whether you are a K–12 educator or a university faculty member or administrator, this work will help you to better understand why PDSs are critical to teacher education and to student learning.

Chapter 2

Managing Knowledge in Professional Development Schools

Carole Basile

Leadership in a professional development school (PDS) takes on certain roles and responsibilities, such as ensuring that PDS goals and initiatives are moving forward, supporting scheduling and fund allocation that provide sufficient support for PDS functions, working toward hiring and retaining a faculty that is uniformly supportive of the functions of a PDS and a school improvement plan, meeting with teacher candidates, and hiring excellent teacher candidates to remain in the PDS. Most importantly, knowledge and systems must be managed in such a way that the resources of the partnership are used wisely to impact P-20 student learning.

Knowledge management is a cousin to intellectual capital. Whereas *intellectual capital* is "the sum of everything everybody in an organization knows that gives the organization its competitive edge," *knowledge management* is "the art of creating value from intangible assets" (Stewart, 1999, p 6). If you think of intellectual capital as a noun and knowledge management as a verb, it will help you understand the importance of the relationship. Every organization has intellectual capital and is interested in growing intellectual capital, but the way to do it is through knowledge management. In a field with increased accountability and educators who are concerned that the complexities of schools is often overlooked and not accounted for, taking stock of both tangible and intangible assets, valuing and managing them, is important for survival and remaining vital in the eyes of the community.

In PDSs, the complexity is compounded by the activities and interactions resulting from the partnership between the school and the university. By defining the assets and giving them value, principals and other

9

school leaders can better articulate the intangible assets and manage them for increased student learning. In Figure 2.1, a group of PDS principals have listed what they believe are the primary intangible assets in a PDS. This serves as a generic list and is not intended to be all inclusive but does address many of the component parts the partnership brings to a school no matter what the level (i.e., elementary or secondary).

This model was organized by adapting the work of Eric Sveiby (2001), an organizational manager whose consulting firm "creates commercial value from knowledge-based assets." Sveiby's model looks at intangible assets from four perspectives: (a) indicators of growth, (b) indicators of renewal and innovation, (c) indicators of efficiency and utilization, and (d) indicators of risk and stability. In addition, each perspective examines elements of external, internal, and human capital. We've used those same four perspectives in creating the matrix of intangible assets for PDSs and students.

Indicators of growth tend to include assets that demonstrate growth of the partnership and growth in perception of the partnership. Indicators of renewal and innovation include assets that demonstrate that programs and people are trying new ways of doing things, reflecting on practice, and implementing new ways of solving problems through external support, internal systems, and human interaction and relationships. Efficiency and utilization mark how well resources are being used and embedded in student learning processes. Indicators of risk and stability track risk factors and how well the partnership leaders are mitigating those factors so that the partnership can sustain itself and thrive.

We have been working with our PDSs to examine what the intangible assets are and how they can be used to communicate the work that is accomplished by the partnership. Three schools are exemplified in Figures 2.2, 2.3, and 2.4. Using the intangible asset monitor as a guide, each school catalogued the intangible assets (based on current institutional memory) they felt were most relevant to the partnership and have had an impact on their school.

What we see in these three examples are schools that have reflected on the intangible assets directly linked to being a PDS. (Schools can create other monitors for other facets of the school, such as other partnerships, the school health in general, or the work of learning communities.) Much of the information is formative for these schools and represents a slice of the current programs and history of each school's partnership. However, each of these schools has a state accountability report, which tells one part of the story, and now an intangible assets "report card" that tells more of the story. They are beginning to manage knowledge that has resulted from the partnership and reflect on how these activities

FIGURE 2.1. Intangible Asset Monitor (Adapted from Sveiby, 2001)

Intangible Assets of Professional Development Schools

External Capital Indicators	Internal Capital Indicators	Human Capital Indicators
Indicators of Growth	Indicators of Growth	Indicators of Growth
• Increasing family/ community outreach projects and programs through the partnership (teacher candidates, site professors, other university faculty) collaborating or interacting with parents and the community • Perceptions and knowledge of parents/ community of the partnership • Communication to parents/ community about the partnership and its mission • Collaborative projects that include all faculty and staff in the school	• Systems for dissemination of information about the partnership • Systems for dissemination of "best" practices or content from the university (i.e., through teacher candidates, site professors, other university faculty) • Systems for recruiting and hiring teacher candidates in the school and school district	• Number of teacher candidates hired over time • Numbers of teachers who are clinical teachers • Numbers of quality teacher candidates • Number of hours teacher candidates are in the school • Number of former teacher candidates in leadership roles • Number of former clinical teachers in leadership roles • Number of teachers taking university courses, workshops, etc.

(*continued on next page*)

FIGURE 2.1. Intangible Asset Monitor (*continued*)

Indicators of Renewal/Innovation	Indicators of Renewal/Innovation	Indicators of Renewal/Innovation
• District involvement in the partnership. (i.e., coordination of all PDS sites by the district) • Number of school faculty who write/present as a partnership in local, regional, and national meetings and conferences about school innovation • Number of activities with other university PDSs that generates new innovation • Number of collaborations across school partners (i.e. businesses, afterschool programs, magnet programs, Ameri-Corps, etc.) • Utilizing partnership resources to create new programs	• Systems for including the partnership resources into planning and school renewal efforts • Systems for including school personnel time to participate in university program leadership • Systems for redefining roles and responsibilities of partnership personnel	• Use of teacher candidate experience and knowledge • Evidence that teachers are reflecting on instructional practice as a result of the partnership (i.e., clinical teachers having teacher candidates, participation in professional learning by the site professor, teachers taking university courses at reduced tuition) • Evidence of inquiry or action research and how it supports accountability processes and best practices implementation

(*continued on next page*)

FIGURE 2.1. Intangible Asset Monitor (*continued*)

Indicators of Efficiency/ Utilization	Indicators of Efficiency/ Utilization	Indicators of Efficiency/ Utilization
• Utilizing partnership resources to increase communication about student progress with families/ community (i.e., service learning projects, parent conference or event participation)	• System for embedding partnership resources in the school improvement plan • Systems for the involvement by the site professor and/or teacher candidates in the hiring process of instructional staff and/or administrators • Space allocation for the partnership • Systems for utilizing grant funding in collaboration with the university partnership	• Utilization of site coordinators' and site professors' direct impact on student learning • Utilization of teacher candidates' direct impact on teacher professional learning (i.e., coteaching, implementation of in-building professional learning, individual connections with students or families) • Utilization of site coordinators' and site professors' direct impact on student learning • Utilization of teacher candidates' direct impact on student learning

(*continued on next page*)

FIGURE 2.1. Intangible Asset Monitor (*continued*)

Indicators of Risk/ Stability	Indicators of Risk/ Stability	Indicators of Risk/ Stability
• District support for funding site coordinator • District support for recruiting and hiring teacher candidates • District support for recruiting and hiring principals and instructional staff committed to the partnership • Perceptions of parents/ community about the partnership	• Systems for collecting data about perceptions of the partnership from faculty and staff	• Number of "problem" teacher candidates • Clinical teacher turnover • Principal turnover • Site coordinator turnover • Site professor turnover • Perceptions of instructional staff • Perception of the principal and other administrators

FIGURE 2.2. Jackson Elementary School (PDS since 1999)

External Capital Indicators

- Teacher candidates created books for 105 students aged 3–5 for a total of 1,365 books sent to students' homes.

- There has been an article about the partnership in each issue of the school newsletter. The partnership banner is hanging in the lobby of the school, and posters provided by the university are posted around the school and in the partnership office.

- Teacher candidates' photos are featured in the main office and as part of the "meet the staff" bulletin board located in the elementary hallway.

- Site coordinator and site professor have made two presentations at the university Action Research Mini-Conference in 2000 and 2001 and published three journal articles and a book about work at Jackson School.

- Through the university Jackson acquired a Title II grant ($9,000) that allowed the school to focus on student voice in curriculum development, mapping of learning experiences provided to students, and overlap of literacy within class offerings.

- Site coordinator and site professor meet monthly with other school district site coordinators, professors, and district and university administrators to create training for clinical teachers and a district model that links teacher preparation in PDSs with induction and retention.

Internal Capital Indicators

- The site professor and site coordinator have developed a system for coaching clinical teachers and teacher candidates as a catalyst for conversation about best practices.

- The school has developed a system for utilization of teacher candidates in the classroom while teachers engage in professional learning community work.

(*continued on next page*)

FIGURE 2.2. Jackson Elementary School (PDS since 1999) (*continued*)

Internal Capital Indicators

- The school has developed a system for including the site professor in the creation of the school accountability plan.

- Systems for technology use have been implemented with a grant funded by the U.S. Department of Education in conjunction with the university. Staff members have been trained, technology is being used beyond word processing for presentation and instructional use, and digital camera use has increased to aid in teaching literacy.

- Systems are in place for clinical teachers and teacher candidates to have lunch each semester for purposes of planning together and introducing clinical teachers to the performance-based assessments of teacher candidates.

Human Capital Indicators

- Five (of 10) elementary teacher candidates have been hired (4 remain on staff); 1 (of 6) middle school teacher candidate has been hired and remains on staff.

- Stability and commitment of clinical teachers:

  o Currently 8 of 10 elementary teachers are clinical teachers; 6 of those teachers have participated in clinical teacher training courses.

  o Five of 6 middle school teachers have been clinical teachers; 1 is currently a clinical teacher and attends the clinical teacher trainings.

  o Five of 15 high school teachers have been clinical teachers; a team of teachers works with any given teacher candidate, spreading the growth opportunity for teachers.

- Three teachers have taken advantage of reduced tuition through the university.

- Eighty-one teacher candidates have been prepared for the school district at Jackson since fall 1999.

(*continued on next page*)

FIGURE **2.2. Jackson Elementary School (PDS since 1999)**
(*continued*)

Human Capital Indicators

- There have been 9 teacher candidates who were dual licensure or special ed–only licensure.

- Coteaching has expanded to allow the clinical teacher to work with small groups or individuals during selected parts of teacher candidates' final internships.

- Stability within the partnership:

  o Same site coordinator for 6 years

  o Clinical teacher turnover as teachers leave the school

  o New teachers eager to participate

FIGURE **2.3. Racer Middle School (PDS since 1996)**

External Capital Indicators

- Teacher candidates and former teacher candidates have joined the school's after-school program in the building and support the district-wide reform initiatives in literacy and math.

- Former teacher candidates are on staff at other district schools and now serve as mentor teachers for incoming student teachers and continue conversations with the site coordinator and site professor in an effort to grow and learn about the art of teaching students.

- Teacher candidates have opportunities to participate in district-level professional development for math, literacy, and special education.

- Experienced clinical teachers have had the opportunity to engage in meaningful conversation with PDS participants from other school districts.

- Former teacher candidates and clinical teachers have taken the study group idea from Racer and introduced it as a form of self-development in their new settings.

(*continued on next page*)

FIGURE 2.3. Racer Middle School (PDS since 1996) (*continued*)

Internal Capital Indicators

- Racer has developed a system of utilizing teacher candidates in classrooms so that currently 14 of 50 staff members are part of an internal study group.

- The school has developed systems for providing all staff members with the results of the study group.

- The site professor and site coordinator have developed a system for utilizing 19 staff members to support weekly professional learning meetings designed for teacher candidates.

- The site coordinator and site professor have developed a coaching system that has now become a learning opportunity for all involved. The debrief process is always done in a triad to include the observations and feedback of the clinical teacher.

- Strategic planning calls for teacher candidates in particular content areas that need the most support.

- Clinical teachers have developed curricular systems so that they now plan units of study and lesson activities around the ability to utilize two teachers in the classroom.

Human Capital Indicators

- Eleven teachers have taken advantage of the reduced tuition credits offered as a benefit of teaching at a PDS.

- The current site professor and site coordinator have been a team for 5 years.

- Nine UCD graduates are now on staff.

- Rock has trained approximately 220 teacher candidates in 11 years.

FIGURE 2.4. Norse High School (PDS since 1993)

External Capital

- Ten school faculty have taught university-level courses.

- Four school faculty assisted in the development of PRAXIS teacher preparation material for university teacher candidates.

- Six school faculty are in leadership positions with the UCD Wyoming Science Inquiry Center.

- North High School teachers participated in the leadership institutes with the National Network for Educational Renewal and were a pilot site for the National Council for the Accreditation of Teacher Educators' PDS standards project.

- School faculty participate in the CU-Succeed program, a program that provides university credit for high school courses.

- The site professor, site coordinator, and other school faculty have published or presented 19 papers/presentations in journals or at national, regional, and local conferences.

- The partnership banner is proudly displayed in the school's lobby, and teacher candidate photos are on the school's Web site.

Internal Capital

- The site coordinator has developed a system for professional development teams that meet during the school day while teacher candidates teach the classes.

- A system has been created for teacher candidates to be involved in data collection and data management for school accreditation.

- The principal utilizes the site coordinator in other roles including school improvement coordinator.

- Systems are in place to include partnership resources in the creation and discussion of the school improvement plan and process.

(*continued on next page*)

FIGURE **2.4. Norse High School (PDS since 1993)** (*continued*)

Human Capital

- Sixteen former teacher candidates are currently teachers.

- Thirty-two faculty received master's degrees as a result of an on-site university–school collaborative.

- Five current faculty members are in the doctoral program at the university.

- The site professor and site coordinator have been a team for 6 years.

- The school has trained over 200 teacher candidates since 1993.

- The university has provided in-school bilingual courses.

and changes may or may not have impacted teacher quality and student learning. This compilation of intangible assets can also be used as a communication tool with the district and the local community about why being a PDS has been important for the school.

These examples also give an overview of the kinds of activities that occur in a PDS in quantitative and qualitative terms, but it is this sense of added value and accountability as a PDS that helps schools realize the contribution the partnership makes. For other schools, especially new PDSs or PDSs with personnel change, the intangible asset monitor helps them consider ways in which the partnership could or should be impacting their school. However, the monitor only provides us with a glimpse of the activities that are taking place in a PDS. In the chapters that follow, we'll take an in-depth look at schools, activities, and projects because behind each intangible asset is a story that wants to be told and helps explain how intangible assets build intellectual capital in a PDS.

Chapter 3

The Principal's Role in Knowledge Management

Cindy Gutierrez and Susan Field

In today's age of accountability in public education, principals no doubt find themselves leading in highly politicized contexts focused on increasing student achievement. From legislation like No Child Left Behind (2001) to the high expectations of school boards and the communities they serve, principals are faced with the immense challenge and awesome responsibility of ensuring that their leadership will ultimately have a positive impact on student learning.

Principals who lead professional development schools (PDSs) have an added layer of responsibility to intentionally plan for and utilize the additional resources the school–university partnership brings (e.g., teacher candidates, university faculty) in ways that support the overall goals of the school. So, what do we know about principal leadership that can be connected to how principals can effectively lead inside a PDS?

In recent reviews of principal leadership literature and research, a common thread throughout indicates school principals are critically important to school success and their leadership matters—it has a profound impact on student achievement (Cotton, 2003; Marzano, McNulty, & Waters, 2005). In order to be most effective, principals need to know where their efforts will have the biggest payoff, and they also need a substantial repertoire of practices or skills to draw upon in order to exercise such influence (Leithwood, 2004). The current research on principal leadership identifies specific responsibilities and practices for school principals that positively affect student outcomes (Marzano et al.). Many, if not all, of the responsibilities are aligned with the four functions of a PDS and are especially critical for PDS principals. Both Cotton and Marzano et al. addressed the urgency for principals to be knowledgeable and highly

21

engaged in curriculum, instruction, and assessment renewal. Research (Cotton, 2003) shows that there is a positive correlation between high-performing schools and meaningful and targeted professional development that enhances instruction; principals of high-achieving schools offer more varied professional development activities than those in lower achieving schools. They are creative in securing the resources—financial, human, time, and material—and facilities the school needs to improve (Cotton). Also, the role of inquiry is aligned with Cotton's research on the critical norm of continuous improvement and the conceptualization of Marzano et al. of intellectual stimulation. Thus, for principals leading full-functioning PDSs, these responsibilities and practices can be actualized through the partnership with the university when principals better understand the intellectual capital of their PDS and can effectively manage and leverage this capital in innovative ways to create value for their school and positively impact student achievement.

Where We've Been: Partner Principal Institute

In an effort to help PDS principals truly understand their unique leadership role as knowledge managers, we created a two-year, eight-session Partner Principal Institute to bring together the principals in our 23 university partnership schools to collaboratively build an understanding of the intellectual capital emerging in their PDSs and how they could effectively identify and intentionally utilize the assets of this capital towards overall school improvement goals. Essentially, the institute provided time and a lens that helped principals see themselves as knowledge managers. What we found to be one of the most important and effective aspects of the Institute were simply the structured and sacred time for principals to engage in conversation and problem solving together. The role of a principal is often a very isolated position with little time to collaborate with other principals. During their time at the Institute, they shared the challenges their schools were grappling with, and at the same time, they shared innovations for how their schools were leveraging partnership resources to try and meet those challenges. From stories of how one principal's site professor had changed the contentious nature of her school leadership team because of the intellectual capital he brought to the table, to ways in which principals were becoming more and more insistent about the use of coteaching among clinical teachers and teacher candidates to meet the needs of students, to the use of teacher candidates to cover classrooms to release teams of clinical teachers for embedded professional development, principals developed not only an array of strategies but also systems to utilize the assets of the partnership. For example, one principal shared how her school was focusing closely on the use of assessment and had just implemented a new assessment team structure whereby a team went in to visit a classroom and collect data and then met with that teacher to delineate noticeable trends as well as brainstorm intervention plans. Teacher candidates had been trained by the site professor and site coordinator to be a part of this assessment team and were gaining significant experience in looking at data in meaningful ways to provide insight into instructional decisions, while adding value to the school's overall focus on assessment.

Where We're Continuing to Go: Developing Unique Spaces for PDS Leadership Groups

PDS Leadership Group Symposium

Although it was important to give principals the unique space to conceptually develop their roles as knowledge managers during the Partner Principal Institute, it also became evident that the distributed nature of leadership in a PDS required new spaces for the key players within the PDS to come together across the university partnership just as principals had done. Although individual PDSs try to embed time for the principal, site professor, and site coordinator to meet fairly often as a team within the school building, the hectic and unforeseen interruptions during a school day often threaten that opportunity to consistently bring these individuals who hold the collective knowledge of the intellectual capital of the PDS together. As a result, we have created a PDS Leadership Group Symposium that has provided an opportunity for all principals, site professors, and site coordinators to come together across the partnership once a year to again collaborate, and develop and share innovative ways in which partnership resources are being utilized. Time is structured so that each group of key players can connect with others in the same role across the partnership to refine the way they think about their roles and to develop effective strategies for carrying out their roles. The leadership groups also meet collectively to talk about the work going on in their schools across the four PDS functions: teacher preparation, professional development, curricular and instructional renewal, and inquiry. Finally, the leadership groups plan together to choose one area of focus, one that is a priority goal for the school as identified in their school improvement plan, and develop an action plan for supporting that goal through the intentional use of partnership resources. Lastly, the group also identifies ways in which data can be collected to show impact of the work on student achievement. Figure 3.1 shows a template for the action plan.

District-Level Structures for PDS Leadership Groups

As the PDS Leadership Symposium is providing the needed space and time for the key players in each PDS to come together to share ideas across the partnership, we also recognize the unique context within which each PDS is operating. Our PDSs span six urban school districts in the metro region, and although all districts are challenged by common issues, each district also has a unique context and resulting district priorities that influence the work of the PDSs within that district. We have collaboratively approached the selection of PDSs with district administrators so that they, too, can be purposeful about how university–school partnerships can be an intentional resource for the

FIGURE 3.1. Template for PDS leadership group action plan

Identified School Priority/Goal:			
How will we use partnership resources to help us focus on this school priority/goal?			
Action Step	Who Is Involved? (PP, SP, SC, TC, CT, Other)	Timeline	Indicators of Student Achievement We Will Gather
Meeting Dates of PDS Leadership Group to Examine Progress:			

district. Many districts have helped us establish PDSs within particular articulation areas, such that the elementary school(s) selected feed into the middle school(s) selected, which feed into the high school(s) selected. This creates a unique opportunity for the PDS Leadership Groups within a district to also come together to meet frequently to help the PDSs further their work within district priorities, and it allows the university to better understand the context of each district and the challenges they are faced with. Currently, we have established this district-level meeting structure in two districts. The meetings include the PDS Leadership Groups from each PDS in the district and the university director of teacher education and a district administrator who serves as the district liaison for the university partnership. This not only provides an opportunity for PDS Leadership Groups to continue to focus on the action plans they developed in the partnershipwide Symposium, but it also creates space for continued conversations of renewal and collaboration between the university and the district. We are currently working with the remaining four districts to establish similar structures.

Conclusion

Based on Hargreave's (2003) notion that schools are only effective to the extent that they can mobilize resources to make an impact, it is essential that school–university partnerships be strategic in developing a plan for knowledge management of the intellectual capital of the partnership. Hussi (2004) concurred: "Vision and strategy are essential for intellectual capital because it can only exist and be developed in the context of an organization's strategy. In other words, intellectual capital does not exist without leadership" (p. 38). Continued innovation in our approaches to collaboration with our PDSs and partner districts will be crucial to truly having a meaningful impact on student learning.

Chapter 4

Building External Capital
Reaching Out to the Community

In many schools, its status as a professional development school (PDS) is its best-kept secret. The community may or may not know that their school is a PDS, and many communities don't really know what a PDS is. Murrell (1998) pointed out that the concept of the PDS must be extended and elaborated in order to respond to broader social, political, and cultural concerns. Building external capital means that (a) the entire community (i.e., all school staff, parents, business partners, the school district) recognizes and participates in PDS activities; (b) relationships are built between the university partners (teacher candidates, site professor) and the community, and each recognizes each other as vital to the success of students; (c) support is provided for sustainability; and (d) the partnership is recognized and respected locally and nationally.

This chapter provides four stories of how PDSs have built intangible assets through external capital in their schools, communities, and school districts. Each school has done it in a different way. The first, a before-school program initiated by the site professor, has joined teacher candidates and parents in support of literacy skills. The second example describes a teacher candidate literacy project that has reached into the community by providing resources and books for families that do not have access to books in their home. The third story describes a community reading partnership that includes the business community and the partnership in the school's literacy efforts. And the fourth speaks to legacy projects or service learning projects that teacher candidates do for the school as they progress through internships.

Enrichment Through the Fifth Dimension

Honorine Nocon

Intangible asset: "utilizing partnership resources to create new programs"

Founders Elementary School is located in an historic Denver neighborhood made up primarily of single-family homes built in the 1920s and 1930s. Most housing is rental, although the neighborhood is experiencing gentrification as landlords sell the worn properties to upwardly mobile singles and couples. Most residents are Latino, Spanish-speaking, and of low income. Many are immigrants from Mexico. Adult education levels are low, formal education frequently ending at the elementary level.

Founders is a bilingual or dual-language school. Approximately 95% of the children are Latino, more than half of whom speak Spanish as a native language. Overwhelmingly, the children come from low-income households—97% qualify for free or reduced-price lunch.

Founders has been a professional development school for teacher licensure since 1996. The principal and several teachers have supported the partnership for that whole period. Several teachers and the vice principal are products of the licensure program and did their preservice teaching internships at Founders. Currently, more than half the school's staff is serving as clinical teachers to preservice teacher candidates.

This story also exemplifies "The Fifth Dimension," developed in the 1980s by Michael Cole and Peg Griffin at the University of California, San Diego (Cole, 1996, 1999). The name Fifth Dimension refers to the fact that education and learning go beyond the three dimensions of physical space and the fourth dimension of time into the dimension of meaning making. The Fifth Dimension model has its origin in research on the role of culture in child and human development. The more concrete research project that prompted development of the model studied reading disabilities as related to schooling. The original idea was to create an environment rich in learning tools that were designed to promote "the all-around intellectual and social development of 6- to 12-year-old children while introducing them to computers and computer networks" (Cole, 1999, p. 93).

Early in April 2003, colorful feathers began to appear in the hallways and classrooms of Founders Elementary School in Northwest Denver. A black feather even appeared in the principal's hair! Simultaneously, signs appeared in Spanish and English asking things like "Who is El Águila?" and "Did you know that feathers were once used to write?" Children and adults at the school began talking about the mysterious El Águila ("The Eagle") as the children collected the feathers, plucking them from bulletin boards, signs, book cases, and shelves.

A week after the feathers first appeared, children in the third, fourth, and fifth grades received an invitation, in Spanish and English, to come to *El club de escritores* ("The Writers' Club") as part of the Founders Fifth Dimension. Held on Thursday mornings before school, the club was to be a place for using computers to illustrate and "publish" stories that the children were working on in their classrooms. The invitation explained that in addition to being a club for young writers, the Founders Fifth Dimension de escritorios was also a Founders-UCD research project designed to find out how children use computers to write. For a period of 6 weeks, an average of 16 children from the third, fourth, and fifth grades attended each session of the club on a purely voluntary basis. The children typed and illustrated stories from their in-class writers' workshops and wrote to and received letters from El Águila.

The last Thursday of May there was a party to celebrate the children's participation. Children discussed their stories and what they liked about the club with each other, teachers, teacher candidates, and visiting researchers from the Autonomous University of Barcelona, which runs a similar club for Gypsy children.

The 6-week, spring 2003 Founders Fifth Dimension de escritorios was a pilot program, codesigned by literacy coaches and teachers at Founders and the site professor. Based on the success of the pilot, an interinstitutional, collaborative team made up of teachers and literacy coaches from Founders and teacher candidates, doctoral students, and the site professor, as well as visiting doctoral students and researchers from Sweden and Spain, continued running the Founders Fifth Dimension de escritorios during the 2003–2004 academic year. During that time and according to plan, the program evolved. Originally conceived as an auxiliary to the school district's mandated classroom literacy program, later versions of the club used Kid Pix and other content-open, art-based software to enhance children's writing by providing guidance and encouragement to participate in the practices of writers.

The program as of spring 2004 reflected ongoing evaluation and refinement based on input from Founders teachers and children and teacher candidates and doctoral students from UCD. Teacher candidates participated, creating materials and incorporating an approach to working with literacy based upon their diverse classroom experiences at the school. The librarian–computer teacher facilitated the expansion of the program to include Tuesday afternoons and participated regularly. Teachers in the second grade brought or referred children who could benefit from extra attention to their writing, and the program expanded to include that age group, as well as the younger siblings of older participants. Children and staff at the school continually referred to the club as "Águila's Club" or "Águila's Writing Program," so the name was changed to "Aguila's Writers' Club." Feathers continued to appear around the school, and children wrote to El Águila in some of their classrooms, later bringing the messages to the club to deposit in the "air mail" box. Children and teachers knew that El Águila would always reply.

As noted in the introduction to this volume, the most important questions asked in any research on PDSs concern impacts—"impacts that produce improved student learning outcomes; improved preparation of preservice teachers, administrators, and other educators; and improved, continuing professional development and learning for all school-and university-based adults who work in the partnership (Teitel, 2000, p. 11)." The Fifth Dimension at Founders had impacts for all these groups as well as on the school itself. It did so by systematically integrating external intellectual capital with internal intellectual capital and human resources.

Links to External Capital

The Founders Fifth Dimension de escritorios provided an immediate link to external intellectual capital in two ways. First, the site professor engaged teacher candidates and doctoral students in participation in the program. One of these students, who was director of instructional technology at a higher education institution, brought technological expertise to the school and participated on the school technology team. Another was a postsecondary instructor of Spanish who brought expertise in bilingualism and biliteracy (which were also areas of expertise for the site professor). Another doctoral student was a teacher at the school and effectively embodied a link between the doctoral program and the culture and expertise within the school.

The second link with external intellectual capital was through the networks of teachers, teacher educators, and researchers who worked with the Fifth Dimension in more than 40 international university–school partnerships. Visiting researchers and graduate students from Sweden and, particularly, Spain, have been working with the children, the teacher candidates, and Founders teachers since the Founders Fifth Dimension de escritorios began.

The Impacts of El Águila

Perhaps the most surprising impact of the Founders Fifth Dimension de escritorios has been the coconstruction of the mysterious El Águila. Based on an element of the Fifth Dimension model and Founders' mascot, the Founders Eagle, El Águila, was introduced through signs, a mail box, and very sketchy references. El Águila was coconstructed in conversations at the school, and El Águila existed in the shared imagination of Founders' children, teachers, teacher candidates, and other adult participants in El Águila's Writers' Club. Evidence of El Águila's presence and participation came from colorful feathers people found around the school but also in the form of responses to letters written by the children. If a child wrote in English, the response was in English; if a child wrote in Spanish, the response was in Spanish. The grammar and spelling in a child's letter was corrected only passively, by modeling the correct form in the response. While labor-intensive for the site professor and doctoral students who shared the role of El Águila in writing those timely responses, correspondence with El Águila emerged as a central activity in the Founders Fifth Dimension de escritorios, and as noted above, spread to the classrooms and school halls, impacting school culture.

For teachers at Founders, some of the impacts of the Founders Fifth Dimension de escritorios were increased attention for their referred students by adults in an informal bilingual learning environment and exposure to software and its use in language and literacy learning in ways that complement classroom practice.

For teacher candidates at Founders, participation in the Fifth Dimension has provided a basis of comparison between teaching and learning in grade-based classrooms and collaborative, exploratory learning in a cross-age informal bilingual learning environment in which they get to know more children from Founders under different circumstances.

For the children at Founders, the Fifth Dimension has represented an opportunity to participate in learning activities on a purely voluntary basis. Because the ratio of adults to children in the club is higher than in the classroom, children benefit from more individualized attention. While their trajectories through the club's activities are structured, they are also negotiated, giving children the chance to participate in planning their learning activities. Additionally, children, who are asked if they prefer to speak Spanish or English in the club, are regularly called upon to act as child-experts, helping younger or less experienced participants, and often sharing their knowledge with participating adults. As one child who regularly participated put it when asked what she liked about the club, "[I like] that the Aguila sends us all cards and we can write on the computer, and write a story."

The Prompt & Present Club

Denise Kale and Donna Sobel

Intangible asset: "utilizing partnership resources to increase communication about student progress with families"

> Fox Elementary mirrors the realities present in many of today's urban schools: 40% of the 538 students are from minority backgrounds, 80 students (15%) are identified with special education needs, 74 students qualify for English language learner (ELL) services, and the school has a 29% student mobility rate and has a 93% attendance rate falling below the state goal (95%). The site coordinator, site professor, teachers, and teacher candidates coordinated an effort to reduce absences and tardiness at the school by reaching out to families in a new way.

It was mid-September as the 40 staff members at Fox Elementary school shuffled into the media center for an after-school faculty meeting. After a few "care and concern" updates regarding a second grade teacher recovering from an unexpected surgery and introductions of a new paraeducator working in the computer center, everyone's attention was directed to the day's one and only agenda item—the lack of adequate annual progress that students in our building were making. As the principal pointed to a table of student performance data on prepared handouts, she commented on a few particularly concerning patterns. A snapshot from one primary class revealed that only 14 of 22 youngsters were on target for the state-defined goals of adequate yearly progress in reading. Early projections from one kindergarten classroom suggested that only 4 of 16 students were on target for a year's growth in writing.

The collective sighs heard throughout the room resembled those of our students during a standardized testing session. Comments that began to surface seemed to capture the frustration of staff, "It seems like every day I have to begin by saying, 'Unfortunately, since so-and-so didn't hear the explanation yesterday, let's go over it again.'"

Another teacher echoed a similar concern: "I feel that I am always backtracking. I don't even think that a review is sufficient, rather I need to totally teach yesterdays lesson before I can start with today's."

The general sentiment appeared to be that teachers shared not a defensive stance on this important issue but rather an explanatory posture best summarized by one teacher's question: "How can we teach these kids, if they're not here?"

Driving home from that meeting, I began to ponder how I might be of assistance. I knew I was in a unique situation this school year. As a teacher in the school district, I truly understood the demands my colleagues were feeling. They were all involved in intensive professional development efforts aimed at the new literacy and mathematics curriculum and were continually reminded that they worked in a low-performing school.

I had a conversation with the building principal the following day, and we agreed that the current practices regarding problematic attendance (computer-generated letters sent home followed by an interagency meeting aimed at brainstorming alternative interventions) were punitive and clearly not contributing to improved attendance rates. With her encouragement to investigate this topic, I turned then to a literature search to help generate other possible solutions to our attendance challenges. From that reading, a number of potential suggestions surfaced that meshed with the current building and community culture. Those included the following:

- Design a plan that is multidimensional. Attendance is a complicated issue, hence create a broad approach that ensures that all of the stakeholders involved in this important issue are also meaningfully involved in the solution.
- Create a gathering known as the "100% Club," a special gathering where anyone with 100% attendance is invited for a celebration.
- Provide classroom privileges (e.g., line leader) for those with improved attendance.
- Create an ice cream social family event where improved attendance is acknowledged.
- Make a concerted effort to get to know the student as well as his or her family and the issues surrounding the attendance issue.

This means making phone calls home when signs of improvement are noticed, genuinely asking, "What can I do to help?" or inquiring about bedtime routines.

- In written formats, in person, or over the phone, take the opportunity to provide advice to the student and his or her family members on techniques for getting to school on time.
- Create an incentive system for whole classes to get rewarded for improved attendance.

Our Plan for Improving Attendance

With those suggestions in hand, the administrative team prioritized a number of strategies that more personally honored the values and goals of the Fox School community and presented the plan to the faculty. This plan was overwhelmingly embraced by staff. In an effort to maximize the benefits of the university partnership, our plan to improve attendance and tardiness was underway with the following:

- *Whole school effort.* Color-coded bar graphs were created from large poster board and prominently displayed in the school's front hall comparing 2 months of attendance and "on-time" data. Several intermediate teachers used these graphs in their daily math lessons.
- *Whole class incentives.* Each day's school announcements included an attendance message. We announced those classes that had perfect attendance the day before over the intercom. Every trimester, the class that had the best attendance record received a pizza party.
- *Individual acknowledgments.* Each month, class lists of students' attendance and promptness were distributed to teachers. Together, the principal and every teacher planned and copresented a monthly attendance discussion in each classroom. Students who had been on time to school and those with perfect attendance received a special privilege (first in line for lunch), perfect attendance certificates, bookmarks, pencils, and, for those earning perfect attendance for more than one month, a certificate for a free book from the school store. Classroom teachers shared those monthly statistics with their students and included this information in monthly newsletters sent home to family members.

- *The Prompt & Present Club.* After a thorough analysis of school-wide attendance data, 50 students demonstrating chronic tardies and poor attendance where selected for participation in our newly designed Prompt & Present Club. Together the site coordinator, site professor, and a group of eight teacher candidates served as the lead facilitators for small groups of five students. Each week, the teacher candidates received a report of their students' attendance and tardies. They then scheduled and met individually with the student to set personal goals for improving attendance and reducing tardies. During those weekly sessions, teacher candidates used scripted prompts to help establish rapport while strategically addressing those attendance issues. Once per month, the entire club came together for a celebration of successes. Additionally, the teacher candidates regularly called parents of the Prompt & Present Club students to encourage support for attendance and to congratulate them when progress had been made. Lastly, family members of the students in the Prompt & Present Club were invited to two dinners at the school where they met personally with the teacher candidates. Fox's principal used this forum to discuss the importance of coming to school and being on time as an essential life skill.

Successful educational initiatives often involve the participation of many members. The university partnership quickly surfaces as key to this project. Collaboratively with school personnel, the teacher candidates hosted the school–community dinners. They assisted in securing donations from a local grocery store to cover food as well as donated alarm clocks from another nearby store. Other local businesses assisted by contributing gift certificates for free meals to students achieving improved attendance.

Project Findings

To measure the effectiveness of this project, we analyzed the trends in student attendance data and surveyed teachers and teacher candidates to understand how they felt about the project.

Schoolwide Attendance and Tardy Data

Each month, attendance and tardiness information was gleaned from the district database. This project appeared to have a positive impact on students getting to school on time. End of school year data was compared to beginning of school year data and revealed that tardies were reduced by 51%. When compared to the previous school year, overall tardy patterns were reduced by 3%, with schoolwide attendance increasing by 1.3%.

Prompt & Present Club Attendance and Tardy Data

The Prompt & Present Club began in October with 54 members. Five of those students moved over the course of the school year. Of the remaining 49 students, 25% are currently receiving special education services, 29% have an individualized literacy plan indicating they are reading below grade level, and 51% were identified by their classroom teacher as not being "on track" for making adequate yearly progress. Clearly, this is a group of students in need of support services. These students demonstrated significant improvement in coming to school on time. Tardiness rates decreased by 68% during the 7-month period of October to May. However, attendance did not improve. In fact, there was a 14% increase in unexcused absences by members of the Prompt & Present Club during the same 7-month period. An analysis of individual student data revealed a clear pattern of improved attendance for students in grades 3–5, yet an alarming number of unexcused absences for students in grades K–2. In general, we were more successful in increasing attendance with older students. It is understood that younger children are of course more dependant on their parents for getting them up, fed, dressed, and taken to school.

Link to Building External Capital

The initiative to improve attendance and tardiness illustrates how the lofty aims of a university–school partnership can be realized through collaborative efforts of university, school, family, and community members. Even though the results were not as successful as the school wanted in the first year, there was success and an outreach program was in place to continue striving for increased attendance. Genuine and meaningful partnerships such as the one between Fox School and the university demonstrate how students most in need can be reached and how external capital can be built through ongoing relationships with students and families. Working together, initiatives such as the Prompt & Present Club show students and their families that their school community values their presence at school, teacher candidates recognized the importance of getting to know families and understand their hardships, and teachers realized the impact they could have on the community's culture.

Connecting the Community Through Literacy

Flo Olson, Heidi Bulmahn Barker, and Mike McGuffee

Intangible asset: "increasing family–community outreach programs and projects through the partnership"

> Jackson School is a unique public school of choice with a 30-year history and students who come from all over the Denver metroplex representing a variety of cultures and socioeconomic levels. The school constituents include prekindergarten through 12th grade students in mixed-age classrooms through high school. It has a nongraded, individualized, challenge-based curriculum. In this project, teacher candidates and teachers worked with a site technology expert to use a technology innovation called RealeBooks so that all students would have access to books.

What if one child were offered an endless supply of engaging texts to read? And what if that child were invited to add to that supply by sharing experiences through writing books of his or her own? What if adults within our community were taught to create publications using digital photographs of familiar people and places, inviting others to share their experiences, their homes, their cultures, and their perspectives? What if every preservice teacher had the experience of being an author engaged firsthand in the writing process? What would *that* mean to the literacy of our community?

These notions have challenged us to examine literacy within our school community. Based on the belief that not all our families have equal access to appropriate and meaningful books for their children, we have elected to embark on an e-publishing project. Our teachers, teacher candidates and students are engaged in the creation of e-books called Webbes. We use digital cameras, laptops, and high-speed printers (tools that we have invested in during the partnership) to distribute our creations to our youngest readers and their families.

Our first goal is to create e-books that can be distributed on a weekly basis to our preschool and kindergarten families. Several of our teachers and students are creating books that are used by the kindergarten teachers. Additionally, each teacher candidate created an original book used in the project. Each e-book becomes part of an e-library—a resource for future printing and a legacy left to the school and the community.

The Book Cycle and the Professional Development School

In our professional development school, we focused on this question: What if preservice teachers became authors, fully engaged in the writing process, and produced books for the 79 preschool and kindergarten students at the Jackson School? We utilized the book cycle (i.e., creating, producing, distributing, and valuing) as our framework for the process.

Creating

Our first task was to educate the 11 elementary teacher candidates doing their internships at Jackson. Some were beginning their final internship, and others were just beginning the teacher education program. As a group, they had a diversity of experiences and knowledge about literacy. The site professor, the site coordinator, and school administration met and decided to set aside about $3,500 out of general funds for the project. This would include not only the supplies needed but also time for teacher professional learning with a literacy and technology consultant.

At this time, each PDS had a site technology expert through a U.S. Department of Education Preparing Tomorrow's Teachers to Use Technology (PT3) grant. This "site tech" was a former site professor at Jackson who also had his own literacy consulting business that helped schools and other organizations create digitized books for children and families. In this project, he was responsible for enhancing technology at the school and working with teacher candidates and teachers to integrate technology into their instruction. Typically, the site tech was in the school one day per week. The site tech, one of the creators of Webbes software, conducted four workshops for our teacher candidates. The first workshop consisted of sharing background information about the book cycle as well as looking at trade books published for young and emerging readers. The site tech's invitation was "to understand the book cycle, become a writer, and participate in solving the real problem of solving access to literacy." As teacher educators, we wanted the candidates to learn the writing process from the inside—to understand the process and then be able to guide children through it. We looked at both picture books and "guided reading–type" books. After looking at the trade books, our teacher candidates created descriptors of those books including a close match between picture and text, patterns and repetition of words, predictability of text, topics connected to children's interests and experiences, interesting titles, and features of real books (page numbers, table of contents, index). This led to conversation about how kids pick books and what gains their interest (titles, pictures, fiction vs. nonfiction). We also noticed bright colors and bold text, rhyming, simple themes, one idea or concept per book, consistent placement of text, and a beginning, middle, and end. Some books also gave children the opportunity to be an "instant reader" because of their predictability. We also noted the cost of each of these published books, knowing that cost can be a barrier to building a home library.

The site tech presented a model of balanced literacy grounded in a gradual release of responsibility. The adult models reading and writing, shares reading and writing, guides student practice, and facilitates independent practice. Each step incorporates the idea of collaboration. The goal is always that children will learn to work together and teach each other.

The second workshop focused on learning to use the RealeWriter software. The school purchased software for teacher and student use as part of the project. We met in the computer lab and began to learn the program. Before we dove into the program, the site tech again focused on the value component of literacy, teasing out the components of the valuing of literacy, which most of us in the education field have experienced as a natural part of lives. He told a story about his own daughter and a book she learned to read called *My Puppy*. In this book, every page read, "My puppy." The story was carried by the pictures. First, a little girl is holding a puppy, then a little boy, then his mother, then the father, then other individuals, until the last picture is of the mother dog with the words "My puppy." The point of the story was that his daughter would read the book with all the inflection that makes this story a meaningful book and that reading, if valued, is a joyful experience.

Our third meeting was run as a writer's workshop, beginning with author's chair, where students share their writing with the whole class. Our preservice teachers shared the ideas that they were working on for their own books. Book topics included sports, trucks, trains, planes, space, playing in the snow, feet, sign language, pets, shapes in nature or the school playground, in the forest, in the ocean, months of the year, and "How big?" The site tech encouraged our teacher candidates to think about the concepts of audience and purpose. Our audience is our youngest students and their parents. We posed questions such as, What is it that we want them to take away with them? What conversations might they have? and What connections might they make with the text? After our own sharing, we talked about managing the writing process with kids; the importance of supplies, time, resources, folders, filing systems; and ways to keep audience and purpose at the center. We made it clear that at our next meeting, everyone would come with a draft of their story.

We conducted this workshop in much the same manner: sharing with feedback. The site tech's suggestion to us as we gave feedback was to be careful about micromanaging as we critique, to not rewrite, but rather to ask questions for clarification or to broaden or focus thinking. We also practiced reading the stories as if we were reading to kids, our intended audience. Our preservice teachers continued to work on their books, and we published them as they finished. We arranged open workshop or studio time for them to use the computer lab, and many of them worked at home as the software license included a home copy for each teacher.

Producing

The components of production were ordering supplies, printing, cutting, and stapling. The school already owned a fast, solid-ink printer. This was perfect for this project because of the high quality of color printing and its speed. The printer allowed the Webbes to look like real books, which we know is a component of valuing reading. Other supplies needed were a high-quality paper cutter and a saddle stapler. Paper (28 pound, laser) also contributes to the books looking "real." Color ink is also needed.

As we moved through the process, it became apparent that one person needed to be in charge of the printing process. This person needs to understand the computer and printer and how to troubleshoot. We also realized that time was a factor and that we needed more support in putting the books together. We enlisted middle school students who were looking for opportunities for community service. In the future, parents could be a valuable resource in this task. We also found that our preservice teachers practiced a great deal of skills, such as creating files, downloading software, using digital cameras in the learning process, editing photos, working with software, utilizing thumb drives, and other means of storage and transferring data.

Distributing

Distribution was a bit tricky. We needed to make sure that all students received the right books and the right number of books. It took bags, labels, and classroom tubs to keep us organized. The site coordinator also created a chart that included the name of the book, the author, the reading level, and which classes had received their copies.

Valuing

Much of this process is about creating a home–school connection through books. We began with a book that our site coordinator wrote called *Reading at Home.* This book described this book project, told what parents could expect in the way of books coming home, and gave a brief look at early reading development, with a section entitled "What You Can Do at Home." This book was sent home with the very first Webbe books along with the kids' boxes for storing their collection of books. Before these boxes went home, children practiced getting out the box, opening their box, reading the book, and putting away the box with the book in it. This was done with the support of the classroom teachers, who helped students think aloud about where kids might keep their box at home—a "special place."

Link With External Capital

Webbes are books that reach out to families and provide resources for families that they may not have had otherwise. Jackson School produced over 1,300 books for over 100 students. These were books that students enjoyed reading because they were about their school, their friends, and themselves. The books also built external capital as families were provided with a link from school.

Community Reading Partnership

Betty C. deBaca and Donna Sobel

Intangible asset: "collaborations across school partners"

Alpine Elementary is in an extremely low socioeconomic industrial area. The students are primarily Hispanic (71%) and second language learners (42%). The majority (81%) receive free or reduced lunch. Alpine Elementary School has been a PDS since 1993 and is currently in the process of becoming a Primary Years International Baccalaureate Program school. This story reveals the synergy that can occur when external community funders work along with partnership resources to make a difference for kids.

The new principal at Alpine Elementary had come from a school where the community was very much involved in the educational process. It not only supported the school financially but also brought in much-needed human resources. Having had a successful experience in her prior school, Mrs. Lopez was very excited to have been asked by a prior funder if he could help build programs at the new school. He was very interested in the impact that parental involvement and incentives might have on student achievement. He generously funded an after-school tutorial program for the school but wanted to do more.

The funder came to visit the school and proceeded to present a new idea. He had to see if the principal felt that the idea might be the incentive it would take to make a difference in the state-mandated test scores for students at the third grade level. He was offering to create a Reading Trust Fund for any third grade student who met a challenging, yet realistic, reading goal that had been collaboratively developed by the student's parent(s) or guardian, the classroom teacher, and the student. The fact that this program would be open to all third graders regardless of their language or ability levels was even more inviting. The principal took on the challenge. She really wasn't sure how this program would be set up or how staff would get the parents to "buy in," but that seemed like the easy part. For now, she was just ready to begin.

Because of the successful partnership with the university, the principal approached the site professor and presented the funder's project. They discussed the parameters that the funder had set and what the next steps would be. They discussed how the teacher candidates from the university could be involved in this program and how the implementation of the program could help them fulfill certain requirements from their on-campus course requirements. This seemed like a win-win situation for everyone. Together they created a to-do list, with the site professor assuming responsibility for writing up a written description of the program and the principal working on a timeline that complimented the school schedule. Scheduling a meeting to discuss the project along with an array of logistics with the third grade teachers was at the top of the list.

Under the site professor's guidance, the teacher candidates began preparing for an evening kickoff event. They secured donations from local restaurants for refreshments, books, and small gift certificates to give out as door prizes; set up a book table of recommended literature; arranged for local library to make a presentation and distribute checkout cards; and gathered information for parents on how to help their child read at home. The teacher candidates created invitations to the third grade families and asked for RSVPs to ensure enough food for the children and their families. When it was discovered that they had very few responses from families, teachers were asked to talk with their parents about this opportunity. The night of the parent meeting was very enlightening. Out of a possible 75 children eligible to participate, only 14 attended, and only 2 or 3 were from the classes of the veteran teachers. Possible reasons for this were (a) we had not communicated effectively with parents, (b) the teachers hadn't made follow-up calls, or (c) the parent(s) had to work or were busy with other commitments. We were determined to give every child the opportunity to participate, so the principal asked the teachers to call each parent who didn't attend the meeting and set an after-school meeting to sign the goal agreement and get the program information. With this effort, we gained 29 additional participants. Obviously, there was still more work to do to communicate with families and teachers, but the program was a great success for the students who participated. At the conclusion of the school year, the state test results were reported, and the individual goals were analyzed. Participating students, 29 out of 31, had reached their goal and were honored in a special evening celebration hosted again by the teacher candidates. As parents and other family members proudly took pictures, the superintendent of the school district acknowledged the students' gains, and the funder handed each child a document detailing the trust fund arrangements.

Linking to External Capital

A few days after the awards ceremony, a reporter from a major area newspaper asked to interview the students, their parents, and the teachers. At the teacher interviews, the principal heard the comments the teachers made to the reporter. The teacher whose children participated was very excited about the impact that the incentive had given these children and their families and felt that the program had called attention to the need for parents along with the teacher and most importantly the student to work together on a common goal. When the children were asked what they did to earn the money, they replied they had to identify "main ideas" and write "good paragraphs." They were not only excited that they had earned the money but that they had learned to be better readers and writers.

The school had successfully reached out to the community with the resources provided by the partnership. Not only did the partnership receive attention for their help with the project and events, but the participation of the site professor and teacher candidates illustrated how these resources could also help improve student learning.

A Legacy Can Really Make a Difference

Sherry Taylor

Intangible asset: "collaborative projects that include all faculty and staff in the school"

> Sanchez Elementary School, a professional development school since 1993, provides a linguistically and culturally rich and supportive educational context both for the school-age learners in the neighborhood and for the group of teacher candidates completing their yearlong teaching internship there. Teacher candidates who intern in this school come to understand and respect the harsh realities facing the families of the students—many of whom are American-born, Mexican-American families or recent Mexican immigrant families living in a lower socioeconomic–level neighborhood. In this story, we'll see that external capital does not necessarily have to be external to the school. Often, PDS interaction is limited to those teachers who directly come in contact with teacher candidates. It is critical that the whole school see itself as part of the partnership with the university and that resources are used to support the whole school community.

Teacher preparation and professional development efforts at Sanchez were coordinated by a leadership team that consisted of the principal, a university site professor, a school site coordinator, and five teachers, four of whom had served as clinical teachers to teacher candidate internships. In the initial months of the school year, the leadership team was responsible for (a) reviewing current needs of the school and the school's annual improvement plan, (b) reviewing needs and goals relevant to the four functions, and (c) subsequently generating compatible activities and goals that were also supportive of each of these elements. Each month thereafter, the leadership team met to review issues relevant to progress made toward achieving these goals.

Both the site professor and site coordinator were beginning their second year at Sanchez Elementary. Together with the rest of the leadership team, they generated new ideas and initiatives based on insights gained during their first year at the PDS. In particular, the team identified the need to strategically integrate the goals of the school with the goals and activities of the four PDS functions. As such, the team believed that the potential existed to maximize its efforts and outcomes toward achieving the goals set for the current year. The Legacy Project—a kind of "make a difference" project—offered the potential for a rich integration between the schools' goals and the goals relevant to teacher candidates' preparation, professional development, scholarly and inquiry activities, and use of exemplary practices.

In order to identify a focus for the Legacy Project, the leadership team and teacher candidates separately brainstormed project ideas. Ideas generated by the leadership team included having teacher candidates be involved in (a) the preparation of "teach to" posters for guided reading centers used in the new schoolwide balanced literacy program and related balanced literacy professional development and (b) the schoolwide administration and scoring of the Six Trait Writing Assessment. The teacher candidates generated a sizable list of ideas, including (a) plan and coordinate a fund-raiser for a playground; (b) plan and coordinate an on-site parent resource center with the assistance of the school's parental involvement committee; (c) plan, coordinate, and oversee a science activity night for students and parents; (d) plan, coordinate, and present an informational session for parents regarding standards-based education; and (e) plan, initiate, and coordinate a school beautification club to address playground improvement, care, and recycling efforts. With the site professor mediating, both groups separately reviewed and discussed the individual lists of project ideas. The dynamics were such that the leadership team waited to hear back from the teacher candidates while the teacher candidates actively discussed and weighed the advantages, disadvantages, and realities of each of the seven ideas. The leadership team understood the importance of the teacher candidates having ownership of the legacy project, since they would be coordinating and implementing the related work. On the other hand, teacher candidates wanted to select a project focus that would meet the needs of the school, make a lasting and valuable contribution, and simultaneously provide themselves with opportunities for professional development, inquiry to inform their teaching, and preparation to further their use of exemplary practices in their classroom planning and instruction. Ultimately, the teacher candidates made the decision to select the Six Trait Writing Assessment as the focus for their legacy project. The leadership team was thrilled, especially once they heard the details of the comprehensive project planned by the teacher candidates.

The legacy project the teacher candidates planned and left with the school was twofold. First, teacher candidates made the decision to be involved in the administration and scoring of the Six Trait Writing

Assessment. As one teacher candidate wrote in a reflection, "The idea was to fairly administer and score the test, and then provide a set of scores for the students to the individual teachers and to the school." Additionally, teacher candidates intended to assist the teachers, who were still new to this assessment, to deepen their own understanding of the assessment. Second, the teacher candidates developed a bibliography of Spanish language and bilingual (Spanish–English) children's literature— primarily multicultural children's literature—that could be used across grade levels in preparing students to understand the six traits (e.g., ideas, voice, word choice, organization, sentence fluency, and conventions) in the context of reading and writing. This project met the goals set by teacher candidates and the leadership team, that is, for teacher candidates to make a contribution that would benefit both faculty and students. However, neither the teacher candidates nor the leadership team could imagine how valuable the project would be for laying the groundwork for future professional development opportunities.

In order to assist with the preliminary implementation of the legacy project, the site professor collaborated with the teacher candidates to generate a list of related tasks, to identify the person responsible for each task, and to set a time line for tasks to be completed. Tasks related to the teacher candidates' successful completion of the legacy project included (a) arranging and attending Six Trait in-services; (b) receiving the district writing prompt and administering the Six Trait Writing Assessment to grades 1–5 in a total of 19 classrooms; (c) scoring writing samples; (d) recording and organizing scores by class, grade level, language of instruction, and schoolwide; (e) meeting with each classroom teacher to review individual student scores; (f) planning and delivering presentation of assessment and data to faculty; and, (g) researching and constructing annotated bibliography of Spanish language and bilingual (Spanish–English) children's literature that exemplifies the six traits. Because of the vast and varied nature of the tasks, teacher candidates determined that some tasks needed to be completed by everyone involved, while other tasks needed to be delegated to individuals or small groups. So, while every teacher candidate was involved in each segment of the project, in order to make efficient use of their time the group identified individuals to be responsible for overseeing the progress of specific tasks. Lastly, because the project effort spanned two semesters, the teacher candidates set periodic dates on which they would review their progress, revise and update plans as needed.

Several of the preliminary tasks involved input and collaboration from the leadership team. In particular, the site professor facilitated organizational preparations and the site coordinator made the arrangements for the district representative to conduct the Six Trait Writing Assessment training in-services. Thereafter, the teacher candidates took primary responsibility for the remaining tasks, keeping the site professor and site coordinator updated of their progress and needs through regular e-mail communications. Upon their completion of the in-service sessions, teacher candidates were ready to begin administering the assessment. Teacher candidates found that while the administration of the assessment was fairly simple, the scoring of the writing samples proved to be challenging. Once they realized this challenge was shared by all of them, the teacher candidates decided to meet in the teachers' lounge for 2 days and score together. As such, when teacher candidates were unsure of how to score a specific trait on a writing sample, they were able to confer with each other. As a result, the teacher candidates became fairly proficient and reliable at scoring.

After they completed the scoring task, teacher candidates met with each classroom teacher to review the scores of individual student writing samples. Because the Six Trait Writing Assessment was still new to many of the classroom teachers, teacher candidates were able to first review the assessment, then explain the scoring process and the score for individual students. In most cases, the teacher felt that the scores were fair and accurate reflections of students' writing ability. However, in some cases, teachers questioned individual scores. The review process provided teacher and teacher candidate the opportunity to discuss any discrepancies as well as their reasoning behind a score. Occasionally, the teacher and teacher candidate could not come to agreement. In these cases, they invited a third party to help them make a decision about the score. Through this entire process, teacher candidates honed their skills and understanding of the six traits, the writing assessment, the scoring process, and evaluating assessment data relevant to the writer's needs and subsequent instructional decisions. Ultimately, the teacher candidates tallied and compiled the assessment data in order to provide teachers with a concrete breakdown of the students' scores for the school year, by class, grade level, and schoolwide.

The second part of the legacy project included teacher candidates constructing a bibliography of children's literature that exemplify the six traits. Teacher candidates determined that many good resource books with detailed lists of literature by trait, already existed. Hence, they did not "reinvent the wheel." Instead, they focused on putting together a bibliography of Spanish language and bilingual (Spanish–English) multicultural children's literature. Given their observations of teachers' unsuccessful attempts to locate these resources and given the student population at

Sanchez, the teacher candidates determined the bibliography would be useful in teachers' instruction of writing across grade levels in classrooms where Spanish, English, and both languages were used in instruction. In the bibliography, teacher candidates provided the title of each book, language of the text, a summary, an excerpt, and ways to use the book to assist students in their understanding of the six traits.

Impact on Quality Teaching

Additionally, teacher candidates expressed their positive reactions to the outcome of the project. In written reflections included by teacher candidates in the teaching portfolio they submitted for partial fulfillment of the M.A. degree, teacher candidates commented on the direct benefits they gained from their Legacy Project at Sanchez. One teacher candidate wrote,

> For me [the project] was like a rite of passage in my professional development. Somehow, I just felt "more professional" after this event, as if I had gained some valuable expertise in teaching writing and administering and scoring the Six Trait Writing Assessment.

Another teacher candidate indicated, "Schools in this state will continue to implement this assessment into the curriculum; all of us walked away from this experience with the valuable experience in Six Trait Assessment that will be useful in our own futures." The comments of another teacher candidate confirm this prediction,

This year [first year of licensed teaching], I taught my own students about the six traits of writing, focusing on each as I modeled how to plan, draft, revise, and edit personal narratives. I also read titles from the bibliography that we compiled. Finally, I administered the 6 Trait Writing Assessment to my students first during the fall semester and then again during the spring semester.

And still another teacher candidate summed up the experience by stating,

> Our group Legacy Project was a great stepping stone in my professional development as a teacher. Not only did it help my classroom instruction, but it also opened the door to other professional opportunities. I would not have been able to conduct the conversation [with the Title I teacher] in as professional a manner had I not received the training and had the experience with scoring the Six Trait Assessment. Perhaps more importantly, it helped me realize

that I am a professional educator, one who learns about his trade, shares that learning with his colleagues, and collaborates with them to achieve common goals for the benefit of students.

Linking to External Capital

The final component in the teacher candidates' Legacy Project included presenting their finished "products" at a year-end faculty breakfast meeting. This activity, in as much as anything else, built external capital among all the staff in the school. As they had done all along, teacher candidates shared the responsibilities for the preparation and implementation of the presentation, which they organized by the following topics: (a) general overview of the Six Trait Writing Assessment, (b) overview of the professional learning sessions, (c) review of the scoring rubrics, (d) presentation and handout of compiled assessment data for the student population at Sanchez, (e) guidelines for addressing and integrating the six traits of writing in instruction of the regular curriculum, and (f) handout and suggestions for using the annotated bibliography of Spanish language and bilingual (Spanish–English) multicultural children's literature. Needless to say, the faculty at Sanchez was very appreciative of the teacher candidates' contribution. Not only did the teachers have a concrete breakdown of the students' scores for the school year, they had a rich resource in the bibliography that would assist them in years to come.

The Impact of External Capital

In each of the stories in this chapter, the community benefited from the partnership by receiving services such as after-school opportunities, books, scholarships, or other outreach efforts that brought the school closer to parents, the business community, and other schools locally and nationally. Also, in each of these stories, external capital could not have happened without the internal systems or human capital to make it happen. An after-school program or Prompt & Present Club does not happen without thoughtful planning. Service learning does not have impact unless the volunteers are trained. In this way, as PDSs build external capital, they are also building internal and human capital at the same time.

However, what external capital does that no other part does to create cultural competence, growth, and change is to create a connection with others in the community, by the partnership, and for the partnership. Its outreach of activities illuminates the partnership work for sustainability by making the partnership known beyond the teacher candidate–clinical teacher realm. External capital allows the entire community to be involved in some way so voice can be given to everyone equally and that the partnership can thrive as more and more members are receiving benefit.

Chapter 5

Building Internal Capital
Developing Systems for Managing Knowledge

Internal capital is the systems that are intentionally put in place to manage and utilize partnership resources. Internal capital in a professional development school (PDS) begins with distributed leadership: leadership across the partnership that includes the site coordinator, site professor, teacher candidates, teachers, and administrators. Researchers (Newmann & Wehlage, 1995; Silns & Mulford, 2002) believe that leadership that is *distributed* throughout the school rather than concentrated in the hands of a few individuals can improve student achievement. It is this combined leadership that can develop the systems needed to add value to the school and ensure that partnership resources are utilized for student learning.

The systems created through this distributed process should enable the sharing of knowledge, enculturate, and engage the whole staff about the functions of the partnership (i.e., teacher preparation, professional learning, inquiry, renewal of curriculum) and acknowledge participation in the partnership. For these systems to be put in place, it takes thoughtful conversation with all constituents and an open community that is willing to bring to the table voices that haven't been heard before. If the partnership is to sustain itself and become strategically integrated into the work of the school and the school district, the creation of these types of systems is crucial.

In this chapter, there are stories about a school that has developed a system for hiring teacher candidates as future teachers in that school, the development of a district system for building leadership capacity of the PDS site coordinators through a study group process, the creation of systems for technology that have been employed with partnership resources, the involvement of teacher candidates in a common assessment system being developed by high school classroom teachers, and the involvement of the PDS site professor and teacher candidates in systems of school renewal. In each case, the essay links to an intangible asset from those listed in Table 2.1.

Systems for Growing Our Own

Kathy Prior and John Simmons

Intangible asset: "systems for recruiting, hiring teacher candidates in the school and school district"

> Port Elementary School is a suburban school that prides itself in high achievement and innovative programs. Port has been a professional development school since 1999. Port is a year-round school with four separate "tracks." The school has a student population of 645 students: 85% Caucasian, 8% Hispanic, 3% Asian/Pacific Islander, 3% American Indian, and 2% Black. Over the past 5 years, the system for the selection of new teaching staff at Port Elementary has undergone significant change. Personnel have created systems for enculturating teacher candidates into the school and the school district so that at the end of their internship experience, they look more like second-year teachers than first-year teachers.

Several factors influenced our decision to become a PDS in 1999. As a new school, we enjoyed the energy that was manifested when the efforts of an entire staff were focused on the exciting adventure of creating new ways of schooling. We searched for ways to create a culture of reflection and renewal. We found that teacher candidates provided an atmosphere of inquiry that stimulated the teaching staff to deeply reflect on their practices, there was benefit from a formal relationship with a major urban university, and we grew future members of our teaching staff.

After our first year as a PDS, we recognized the need for a rigorous selection process for our teacher candidates, as we had so many, and choosing was difficult. In order for our teacher candidates to compete for positions, they needed to be highly talented individuals. Our selection process for teacher candidates is as comprehensive as our process for selecting teaching staff. After teacher candidates complete all of the university requirements for admittance to the professional licensure program, we require an additional selection process before we accept them at Port. This process includes standardized teacher-talent interviews (initially, the Teacher Perceiver interview and currently Teacher Insight), as well as site-developed interviews.

After we have selected candidates for our program, staff members expose the teacher candidates to all aspects of our school culture. We are justly proud of our highly functional culture, and we want the teacher candidates to develop a desire to continue at Port as regular staff members. Teacher candidates are exposed to all aspects of our school experience. Most of our teacher candidates obtain a substitute teacher license so that they can substitute teach in our building. They serve on committees, interact with parents, and generally participate in the same range of professional activities as the regular teaching staff. Teacher candidates are observed by administrators and provided with feedback. They participate in mock interviews to prepare them with the skills needed to interview successfully. We are purposeful as we design learning experiences for our teacher candidates in order to create the best teaching applicants for Port Elementary and the school district.

Port Elementary benefits in several ways by hosting the teacher candidates. The school culture has grown to embrace coteaching, modeling, inquiry, and self-reflection. Being a partner school allows these budding teachers to experience school life and its many demands while being guided and supported in professional practice. Our candidates bring novel ideas as well as the latest research to our classrooms and committees and actively participate in school functions. Teacher candidates are viewed by our community and staff as professional colleagues. Working alongside a teacher candidate creates a spirit of cooperation. Teacher candidates serve as a catapult for classroom teachers to become reflective of their practice. Classroom teachers unconsciously perform better, as the "performance factor" of having an observer in the room brings out the best in the teacher. Teacher candidates keep classroom energy levels high, and their enthusiasm is contagious. These eager candidates are pleased to help with the workload, thus lightening the burden of the classroom teacher. Classroom teachers find the teacher candidates quickly learn from modeling and begin to assist with student needs. When asked about the additional time commitment in being a cooperating teacher, these teachers agreed the time investment was minimal compared to the ongoing, reliable, and quality help they receive from the teacher candidate. In our building, teachers now ask for teacher candidates. Those who have teacher candidates don't want to let them go. We value our teacher candidates!

Impact on Students

The benefits of having teacher candidates in the classroom extend to students' learning and perceptions of themselves as learners. When I asked a group of second graders how they felt about having a student teacher in the room, they responded as follows: "They really help out." "If our teacher is unavailable, the other teacher can take the place of our regular teacher." "I can ask questions to whoever is closer." "It's like there are two teachers." "Sometimes I get mixed up, and I forget which one is my regular teacher." Students benefit by having an additional teacher in the room, as this allows for small group interactions and remediation, additional support, and an additional caring teacher to bond with.

Link to Internal Capital

We invest a significant amount of time and energy in our teacher candidates and the systems we use to select teacher candidates to stay in our school and our school district. Currently, 20% of classroom teachers at Port are "home grown." This system builds internal capital for our school and our district. Eighty percent of our teacher candidates have obtained teaching positions in our school district. We are able to advocate with confidence that our teacher candidates are among the highest quality applicants for teaching positions. When we are ready to hire a teacher, our teacher candidates provide a predictable supply of outstanding applicants. This efficiency is a definite asset to our school and district.

Designing Systems for Technology Integration

John Ackelson, Marilyn McIntyre, and Pat Toomey

Intangible asset: "systems for utilizing grant funding in collaboration with the university partnership"

Building internal capital can also involve systems for technology and technology integration throughout the school. Often, new systems emerge from professional learning as one kind of capital builds another. Mountain Elementary is a suburban school with approximately 450 students. Our students range in grade from preschool to fifth grade and encompass a range of diversity in socioeconomic status and race. Students live in suburban, single-family homes, mobile homes, and apartments.

What is unique about the school is our sizable investment in technology. The school opened in 1987 with a specially built computer lab equipped with enough computers for a classroom of students. This lab's hardware has been updated periodically through the years; in addition, the adjacent media center holds a number of computers for student and staff use. Each classroom holds a presentation center consisting of a personal computer as well as a television and CRT (computer monitor or screen), and a basic printer. A large color printer is networked to the classrooms and centrally located in the media center. Other equipment in the school includes a video camera and a digital camera for use in various instructional and noninstructional activities. The school has a Web site (linked to the district Web site) to provide pertinent information regarding the school and district.

Mountain's school district promotes technology use and provides a large data base to store all student test scores, both district and state levels, as well as student report card information. Authorized staff can access information from this data warehouse in a number of ways and download desired information into Excel spreadsheets. In addition to retrieval of test data, district teachers can read demographic information regarding their students through the district's student information system (SASI). This system interfaces with the district's test results, allowing the user to analyze data in any number of meaningful ways. The district also has its own e-mail system and a Web site. Both of these are utilized to facilitate communication and post information.

As one can see, Mountain Elementary has at its disposal a number of technologies and information to support the staff in its process of instructional planning, delivery and implementation, but even with all of this technology available, we found the technology and data were utilized at a low level.

The computer lab is utilized for scheduled classes. All students are rotated in and out to engage in activities supporting various instructional outcomes. This leaves very few times open for teachers to use it with their students outside the schedule. The time a classroom teacher's students occupy the lab is release time for that teacher to conduct planning and accomplish other tasks. The person operating the lab is a noncertified employee who directs the students in the activities primarily designed to increase their skills in accessing information and using the computer for production and word processing, but there is little coordination with classroom curriculum and instruction.

At the beginning of the year, we observed teachers using the presentation stations in the classrooms to check their e-mail and gain access to the Internet and the district Web site. Students used the same equipment as rewards for completing their work. The computer and the television were used to present information in teaching and learning but not in any meaningful way. Nearly all teachers knew how to connect with the district data bank but didn't download the information for organization or their own analyses.

When the teacher candidates arrived for their first internship, they completed a self-assessment, including a skills assessment inventory and an interview, to determine their level of proficiency within the Performance-Based Technology Standard for Colorado Teachers. We found they had good knowledge of how various technologies operated, such as video and digital cameras, personal computers, and calculators but had limited knowledge of the instructional process and how technologies could support this process. The classroom teachers, on the other hand, understood the instructional process but had limited knowledge in applying technologies and the appropriate software.

At that point, the partnership team recognized an opportunity was presenting itself to us. We could establish a focus for training and implementation of the available technology and institute reciprocal teaching among the teacher candidates, the clinical teachers, and the other staff in the school. The teachers could share their expertise in teaching, and the candidates could share their technology skills. In line with the technology standard, we would integrate technology in teaching lesson-plan development, schoolwide assessment, and methods of communication. As the candidates sought the support of the teachers in development and implementation of technology in their lessons, they opened doors for the teachers to see possibilities for technology applications.

Our partnership team implemented three areas of training to support this technology focus, the development of Web sites for teachers, the introduction and implementation of literacy software, and the generation and utilization of information in the instructional process (assessment, diagnosis, instruction, and differentiation). We were fortunate to have money from a technology grant to purchase and install appropriate software in the school's computers to support the training.

We began in the area of communication to train the candidates in Web site development. We chose to use not complex Web site development tools but off-site software, allowing the teacher candidates to focus on content instead of operations and programming. After the class, each candidate was given the charge to develop, in collaboration with the clinical teacher and grade-level team, a Web site for each classroom. The site tech also trained the fifth grade teacher team to use this same software. These teachers helped other teachers and used completed Web sites as models for other classrooms.

The development of the Web sites led to productive interaction among the classroom teachers and the candidates. Together they identified appropriate instructional resources, classroom activities, and strategies to inform and involve parents in classroom activities. At the writing of this article, approximately 60% of the staff has classroom Web sites that link to instructional resources and school and district Web sites. The teacher candidates and their clinical teachers work together to enhance and update their Web sites. Many classrooms are using digital imagery with their Web sites to show examples of student work. They also send their newsletter over the Web site and invite parent responses.

The teachers have received this assistance in building their own Web sites with great enthusiasm. Reciprocally, the candidates have learned ways to communicate information to parents and students to extend learning at home. For example, a second grade classroom put a description of an experiment done at school. The students in this classroom were able to share what they had learned with their families, at the same time reinforcing their own learning by teaching it.

Training for the candidates during a site seminar made use of the available digital imagery and video technology. Operations of digital imagery were presented with suggestions for the applications of using such a technology in classroom instruction. Many ideas were shared during this seminar by the presenters and the teacher candidates, allowing all of us to recognize potential applications of the technology for assessment, differentiation, communication with parents, and other facets of the classroom.

Following this training the teacher candidates began to share their newly developed skills in this area with their clinical teachers, who extended the list of applications we had generated. We observed candidates and staff as they documented student work with digital imagery, some of which they displayed in the classrooms and hallways. They shared images with parents during an open house and parent-teacher conferences. They helped students use pictures in reports, stories, bios, and other literacy genres. They inserted visuals onto Web sites and into PowerPoint presentations. Many classroom teachers were motivated enough to purchase their own digital cameras for use in their classrooms.

Our last round of classes involved the introduction and implementation of literacy software. After we reviewed Mountain's strategic plan and test data, we found ways to support the school's goals for improving literacy achievement. One of these ways was to employ Webbe Reale-Writer software in the school to support the delivery of literacy instruction and applications of the learning by the students. After the software has been installed, it may be used by students to produce their own books and by teachers to produce books for use in the classroom. Because they are so economical, they can be sent home to create libraries in homes, which have few books, if any. It's a simple format including text and illustrations. The illustrations are produced through digital cameras, downloads from the Internet, or internal computer picture files. Actual photographs of student work and real-life situations are used. The students write about each picture in a sequence. Sometimes the text comes first, sometimes the picture. Genres are unlimited, including nonfiction, fiction, poetry, songs, and plays. The books can be published or electronically stored in an online library if the teacher desires.

In the area of assessment, technology was used to access, download, and analyze data. Our site tech coached individual teachers and grade levels as they learned to access the district's data bank. Teacher candidates helped clinical teachers download data and set up Excel spreadsheets. One first grade teacher expressed her surprise and delight at the ease with which her teacher candidate was able to set up a spreadsheet to display data. She can now see herself accomplishing the same task and using spreadsheets to store and manipulate data. It doesn't seem to be the mystery for her that it was before this year.

Other assessment applications have begun. Although time didn't permit specific, focused training sessions for it, much progress was made in formative and summative assessment. As mentioned before, the ability to take photos of students, as they work, as well as the work itself before and after instruction, have many possibilities. Individual student portfolios can be built and stored on computers. Scanners can be used to add copies of artifacts. Anecdotal notes can be stored, then moved to pertinent, appropriate places in the portfolio. The portfolios can be stored in student individual accounts, to be reviewed and expanded. Individual learning goals can be set and responded to by students and teachers to help students learn to practice self-evaluation. Some teachers have begun work in this area and are asking for more coaching and more examples to use.

In this district, report cards are completed online throughout all schools. This was another opportunity for teacher candidates and clinical teachers to learn from each other. As grades and other information were entered by computer, teachers explained the evaluation process, and the candidates helped enter the data. Many teachers still keep all their grade books by hand, and averaging grades is done with calculators and mini slide rules. Entering grades in the report cards by computer is a step teachers aren't too excited about, as they have to balance the grade books on their laps or on a table, using their fingers or a ruler to keep their places. It also takes another step to check that all the grade information has been entered correctly. As teachers make use of electronic grade books and spreadsheets, they will see the advantage of having the report cards as part of the available data on their students. They will be able to access previous year's grade information and test scores for their students. Our candidates have pointed out shortcuts in this process and have helped teachers implement them, and we expect that to occur next year too, since candidates' experience and technology skills are generally at a higher level than those of veteran teachers.

We have observed other uses of technology throughout the building with teacher candidates. One of our teacher candidates worked with each of the students in a fifth grade class to use the National Library of Virtual Math Manipulatives Web site. She forwarded the information to parents with that Web site address, as well as addresses of other Web sites with educational-type games, to help students to develop and reinforce their learning in math and thinking skills at home. This same teacher candidate has been working with students to pull pictures off Google through Web sites so they could use them for their biology project.

A variety of results emerged from a technology focus in lessons. Candidates and teachers began to see how video digital imagery was of real value for assistance in assessment and providing input in the actual instruction. Candidates and teachers began to see how the classroom presentation stations could be used for interactive presentations in place of overhead projectors. Candidates and teachers in classrooms of all grade levels began to discover creative uses of the Internet for research and provide opportunities for differentiation. They began to see the value of a functioning lab that supported their instruction, instead of a place to send students to allow for planning time. As the year progressed, all the candidates at Mountain actively employed various technologies to support their instruction and were addressing their performance-based assessments for technology within the context of instruction.

The students had computer skills they learned through the computer lab and other opportunities at home. This year, though, they had more people in the school to help them and more technology used throughout everyday instruction, so they could advance their skills and see more ways to use them. In addition to the other technology they used, PowerPoint was introduced and utilized by teacher candidates throughout the grade levels. In addition to giving the students one more tool to use for reports, the program helped students organize their information to make more sense of it for themselves and gave them formats to use with other types of assignments.

Technology Performance-Based Standards for Colorado Teachers requires teachers to be skilled and knowledgeable in using technology to support instruction and enhance student learning. The standards' descriptors focus upon technology's use in delivery of instruction and carrying out data-driven assessments of learning. They also specify the expectation that students be instructed in basic technology skills and information be managed and communicated through technology, when appropriate.

Link With Internal Capital

Our partnership team is pleased with the progress we've made in our effort to integrate and integrate technology systematically and intentionally and have identified goals for next year. These goals include giving teachers more technology tools for implementing ongoing assessment and more options for using their presentation centers. We would also like to find a forum for teachers to share successful strategies for helping students themselves use technology to enhance their own learning. We continue to create systems that build internal capital throughout the school, and as we train teachers and teacher candidates together, we are also helping to build human capital for the school district.

Developing Systems for Common Assessment

Beth Hays and Christine McConnell

Intangible asset: "systems for including the partnership resources into planning and school renewal efforts"

> Apple High School, opened in 1963, is a school built on a tradition of excellence in academics and extracurricular activities. Apple is a large comprehensive 4-year high school with approximately 1,700 students. Although there is building in the articulation area, the area feeding Apple High School is experiencing minimal growth.

Most housing is single-family homes, although more condominiums, town homes, and apartments are being built. English is the primary language of most families at Apple. In recent years, there has been an increase in the number of immigrant families, most notably from the former Soviet Union. Overwhelmingly, the students come from middle- and upper middle–income families; only 102 students turned in paperwork qualifying for free and reduced lunch.

Apple has strong ties to its community. Several generations of families pass through the halls of the school and make conscious decisions to return to the area to raise their children and pursue career opportunities. A strong community and its role in creating and sustaining successful neighborhood schools is understood and valued. To emphasize this importance and provide students and staff with an opportunity to proactively and productively engage in community service, numerous outreach programs and partnerships have been established. The school motto, "Excellence is our Expectation," extends to the total community.

In 2002, the staff began to implement schoolwide systems to increase its collaboration and skill base. They became more data driven and are now developing numerous action research programs in English and mathematics, which they believe will positively increase student achievement. All of these efforts focus on Apple High School becoming a professional learning community. In the fall of 2004, Apple decided to become a PDS so that they would benefit from a university partnership and take advantage of the resources such a partnership might bring. In addition, during April 2005, Apple partnered with a local foundation (an ongoing 3-year grant) and the other high school in the articulation area to bring author Robert Eaker to present *Professional Learning Communities at Work: Best Practices for Enhancing Student Achievement* to both staffs. His presentation helped Apple continue to focus on the importance of consistent, rigorous curricula and internal systems for collaboration. Thus, combined with quality classroom teachers and teacher candidates, student data would be utilized to drive instruction.

As teacher candidates intern at Apple High School, they learn about professional learning communities within the school. At Apple High School, clinical teachers try to model this theory for the teacher candidates. The school has created a system whereby all of the teacher candidates at Apple High School participate in a learning community. As members of the learning community, they have the opportunity to collaborate with the teachers, share instructional strategies and assessment ideas, and engage in data analysis conversations. The example that follows exemplifies how the school has included everyone in their professional learning communities and how they have melded the partnership in everything they do.

One day, the algebra content team determined the scope and sequence of the semester, based on the essential learning for the algebra classes. The team also identified what standards need to be addressed. Once the semester was outlined, the team then discussed best practices in teaching. On this particular team, one of the teacher candidates participated in this discussion. She provided the team with new, innovative ideas to teach algebra to students. The algebra team also took time to discuss the development of the common assessments, as well as the outcomes they would like to see in student achievement. The first common assessment of this content team was designed by a teacher candidate, in conjunction with performance-based assessments required by the licensure program.

After the common assessment was given, the team came back together again and discussed the data from the assessment. They discussed what common trends took place in their classrooms, good and bad, and then compared the feedback to see if this was the same in other classes. Ultimately, the team was discussing if the student knew the information and how the test confirmed this.

Another aspect that was helpful for the team and the teacher candidate was hearing what strategies other teachers used to teach certain topics. It was then interesting to look back at the assessments and see what strategies really seemed to work for kids and really helped them learn. More importantly, it has allowed the teachers and teacher candidates to understand that it is OK to reteach a concept in a different way to ensure that the students are successful.

Links to Building Internal Capital

Creating systems that utilize partnership resources into planning and school renewal efforts is a significant indicator of internal capital. The teacher candidate in the math department had the unique opportunity to provide leadership and expertise during the discussions leading up to the formal development of the common assessments for algebra. In addition, the teacher candidate developed one of the common assessments that is now used by the department. The focus on data-driven instruction and its impact on student achievement is an ongoing process at Apple. The inclusion of work by teacher candidates and the partnership in departmental projects has been a positive experience.

Building Systems for a Community of Practice

Jane Tarkington and Phillip A. White

Intangible asset: "systems for including the partnership resources in planning and school renewal efforts"

Millennium Elementary is an urban school located in a northeastern suburb of Denver. Millennium's enrollment is currently 536 students. The school serves a diverse, mobile population of students from a variety of backgrounds. Hispanic students make up 75% of the enrollment, while 13% are African American, 7% are Caucasian and 4% are other races. The majority of the students are of low-income families who speak Spanish as a first language. Approximately 80% of the students receive free or reduced-cost lunch. Millennium has been a University of Colorado at Denver and Health Sciences Center professional development school for teacher licensure for 8 years.

The school district and building-level administration have strongly supported this partnership. At present, 14 out of 25 classroom teachers are products of the licensure program and did their preservice teaching internships at Millennium. Currently, more than half the school's staff is serving as clinical teachers to mentor preservice teacher candidates. The school and the school district have systems in place to assist schools with renewal processes. At Millennium, the site professor and teacher candidates are an integral part of those systems.

A Site Visitation and Evaluation

In early February 2005, there was a site visit to Millennium by several high-level district administrators, including the district superintendent and some out-of-state educational experts in the field of school renewal, who met with the school principal, instructional coaches, and teacher leaders. The purpose of the visit was to determine evidence of district leadership goals for staff development within individual classrooms. The visitors were planning to visit several classrooms of various grade levels in order to get an overview of the entire school. As the visitors progressed through a fifth grade class, one of the out-of-state experts engaged a student who appeared to be struggling through a math problem. The expert leaned in and directly explained to the student how to solve the problem. Later, during the debriefing with the district administrators and Millennium staff, it was strongly recommended that the teaching staff needed to demonstrate more direct, explicit teaching.

The next day, the majority of the teachers at Millennium had heard about the recommendation and expressed varying degrees of indignation. It was commonly viewed that the visitors had failed to understand that Millennium staff emphasized problem solving as a teaching strategy and that what the out-of-state visitor deemed problematic had been viewed by the classroom teacher as evidence of the student engagement with an appropriate problem-solving activity. Still, the math and literacy teacher leader coaches found that they were all not in agreement as to what constituted explicit instruction and decided that they needed to rebuild common understandings of what constituted explicit instruction. They began pulling down texts from their office bookcases and rereading about explicit teaching, comparing the writings of the text to their own understandings of explicit teaching, and discussing with one another the relationships between explicit teaching and problem solving.

By mid-February, at the leadership team meeting, the question of what constituted explicit teaching was discussed, and it was decided that the entire teaching staff could benefit from renewing individual understandings of explicit teaching, as well as coming to a stronger, building-wide common understanding of explicit teaching. The principal and the leadership team, through collective mediation (Borko, Wolf, Simone, & Uchiyama, 2003; Coburn, 2006; Cobb and McLain, 2006; Grossman, Wineburg, & Woolworth, 2001), systematically gathered and evaluated current writings on explicit teaching.

For the last 7 years since the initiation of the teacher internship as part of the partnership with the university, teacher candidates have been included as a continuous part of the entire professional school development program at Millennium. While initially the teacher candidates were merely peripherally involved (Lave and Wenger, 1991) in these staff development activities, as they progressed through their teaching internship the candidates assumed greater and greater participation and responsibility within these activities. So that by the middle of March, when the entire teaching staff was engaged in deeper understanding of explicit teaching the teacher candidates were active participants in constructing common understandings of explicit teaching.

Internal Systems

Millennium faculty describes themselves as a forward-moving school and a community that accepts responsibility, solves problems together, and values professional development where teachers collaborate as lifelong learners. It is rare to find conversations in which parents are blamed for the pedagogical challenges often presented by students who have grown up in poverty, speaking a second language. Instead, there is an emphasis on professional development and collaboration rather than teaching in isolation. The staff at Millennium shares a core of common beliefs and understandings about student learning that are evidenced in shared graphic organizers around such constructs as the teaching–learning cycle, the writing process, the reading process, and the "scaffolding for independence," to name a few. The priorities of the student achievement are critically linked and driven by the collection and analysis of data at all levels in the system—student growth, teacher professional growth, teacher candidate professional growth, and whole school progress; the whole is linked to district support. High standards and expectations for both students and teachers are centered on student learning. Professional learning embodying National Staff Development Council Standards is results driven and embedded in teachers' daily work.

As is common, Millennium develops a school improvement plan (SIP) based upon the review of data collected for that school. The SIP prioritizes expectations for student achievement, staff professional development needs, and plans for increasing parental involvement. School improvement plans are the basis for measuring the progress of each school and each student through the continual, ongoing collection of data. Plans are developed, implemented, and monitored by the building principal and the building leadership team, and all teacher candidates are familiar with the SIP, and all instructional lessons, even those mandated by university course syllabi, are constructed around student academic needs and learning.

The professional development and leadership structures and processes inherent in the district initiative have been at the center of Millennium's work for over a decade. Teachers' professional development, and thus teacher candidates' professional development that supports student learning, has been germane to the school culture. Through high-quality, ongoing, job-embedded professional development, teachers and teacher candidates have multiple opportunities to collaborate, observe, and analyze student work and conduct informal action research. Collaborative structures and activities include regular staff in-service days, weekly buildingwide dialogue meetings, weekly team lunch meetings, monthly grade level team meetings, quarterly data conferences, and professional readings. Staff members are expected to regularly write individual action plans to set goals for their individual growth in math, literacy, and language acquisition. The teachers are coached by expert teacher leaders through focused classroom observations and a one-on-one instructional dialogue that follows.

The members of the Millennium leadership team are highly representative of the entire faculty and include the principal, assistant principal, affective educator, English language acquisition coordinator, primary demonstration classroom teacher, intermediate demonstration classroom teacher, site professor from the university, and the site coordinator employed by the school district to support the professional development of the teacher candidates. Other members are three math teacher leaders and three literacy teacher leaders who coach half-time and teach in their own classrooms half-time.

Building Capacity Through Community of Practice

Teachers' understandings, attitudes, and behaviors are central to teacher candidate learning. As this narrative about explicit teaching makes evident, how an effective educational setting responds and commits to the assessed needs effectively models for the teacher candidates and classroom teachers ways to improve student achievement. Through the shared practice of classroom teachers, the teacher candidates as newcomers gradually appropriate the teaching practices of the more expert classroom teacher and over time become full participants in educating the students of Millennium Elementary. So in the middle of March 2005, classroom teachers and teacher candidates each had a copy of Gerald Duffy's *Explaining Reading* (2003) when they met together to build shared understandings about explicit teaching. The agenda on the board was posted, and staff and interns broke up into small study groups. There they worked together on explicit instruction in explaining concepts about reading, vocabulary, fluency, comprehension strategies, and word recognition. They deepened their understandings about scaffolding assistance and its relationship with explicit instruction. All of this has been organized and structured through the attentive presence of the teacher leaders of the school.

In mid-April there was another site visit; this time the directors of curriculum and instruction were the visitors who met with the building principal and leadership team members. As they visited some classrooms, they focused on math instruction, to determine if the math activities were open ended and rigorous. In other classrooms they observed small reading groups to determine evidence of explicit instruction. During the debriefing, the evidence of explicit teaching was analyzed, and two questions were raised to narrow our focus around explicit teaching: Are we getting our kids to think strategically? Are we planning cohesively enough with our special education teachers?

However, the question is raised: "Why explicit teaching in literacy? Wasn't the issue raised about a need for explicit teaching in math?" Based on state-mandated yearly achievement tests, as well as school district yearly assessments, the students at Millennium have usually achieved one or two of the highest math scores in the district, far out-performing schools with similar socioeconomic and second-language populations. In studying about explicit teaching, the staff decided that it was in literacy that the students could best benefit from explicit instruction, not in math.

Link to Building Internal Capital

At Millennium Elementary, teacher candidates enter the professional practice of experienced teachers as newcomers, peripheral to the activity of teaching, and after 800 hours of internship move into the ranks of first-year teachers with a rich, complex experience that supports a strong foundation of intellectual capital for becoming a classroom teacher of great professional expertise. This foundation of intellectual capital is constructed and mediated through participation with the entire school community in classroom teaching practices, staff development that involves the entire building faculty, on-site seminars that focus on teacher candidate individual needs, and the provision of communication links between classroom activities, building activities, and university activities that support the entire system and relationship of partnership schools.

Over a 3-month period in early 2005, incremental change was made within the shared understandings and teaching practices of the staff and interns at Millennium. Through questions posed by those outside of the immediate Millennium community during the site visit of early February, there was initiated an ongoing recursive exchange of building intellectual capacity within the community. For the teacher intern, it is of critical importance to be working closely with the clinical teacher, both in the classroom and at staff development. However, it is the internal systems that are in place, including active leadership teams, weekly buildingwide dialogue, book study, shared constructs of learning, and engagement in staff development, that create the coherence of the community practice.

And finally, it is the attentive presence of multiple individuals who on a daily basis make sure that the incremental, daily work of school gets done. All of these activities, and more, contribute to the ongoing building of professional capacity of the staff at Millennium, which in turn supports strong student academic achievement. By April, teacher candidates were writing in their lesson plans notes regarding explicit teaching for their literacy lessons. They were becoming full participants in the profession of teaching and education.

Evolving Roles: Relationships and Policy

Heidi Bulmahn Barker and Caron A. Westland

Intangible asset: "systems for redefining roles and responsibilities of partnership personnel"

> Systems that build internal capital don't always happen within one professional development school. In a fully functioning partnership, systems are also built across PDSs, especially across site professors and site coordinators within a school district. In this case, roles and responsibilities are being redefined and reshaped so that the district can begin to use the PDSs as a resource for the district. In addition, the school district has developed a model for utilizing PDSs across the district and developing systems for linking teacher education with recruitment, induction, and retention.

We are living, working, and learning in a time of funding cuts and lower school district enrollments, as well as a time of school accountability. Even though most aspects of the partnership are clearly valued and supported through learning in both the public school setting and the university setting, fiscal issues become a challenge. Historically, funding personnel typically creates some interesting dynamics between the district office and a professional development school. For example, in our model, where every school has a site professor funded by the university and a site coordinator funded by the school district, it is often the case that we have to become very creative about who the people are and how the work gets done without invalidating the relationships between the school district and the university.

In this particular school district, every elementary school, including the four PDSs, had a half-time instructional coach, and each PDS had a site coordinator. When money was available, financing the instructional coach and site coordinator positions was not problematic. Economic constraints, however, caused the district to reevaluate the budgets and financing of those particular instructional support personnel. The district decided that the instructional coach role was similar or should be similar to the site coordinator role and decided to merge the two roles. Upon examination of the merger of these two jobs, we soon realized that the task of combining the roles of instructional coach and site coordinator was approached differently by each school. The different approaches were influenced by the person who was to assume the new role. Their previous job functions impacted their interpretation of the new combined role. For example, in one school, the site coordinator or instructional coach had previously been a full-time site coordinator and now added the instructional coach responsibilities. In two other schools, the previous full-time instructional coaches added the site coordinator roles. In the other school, the two jobs continued to be separate titles and roles. This chapter describes the process of how we studied the impact of combining the instructional coach position with the site coordinator position at the PDSs. We also examine the differences between that new role and the discreet titles that are described in the original PDS model our university and school partners based their partnerships upon.

Studying the Evolution

Each month, usually for a half day, the site professors, the site coordinator, and site coordinators or instructional coaches participated in districtwide "instructional coaches' study teams." Approximately 20 teams, each with five to eight instructional coaches, met together to discuss relevant topics. In these meetings, the groups discussed issues related to their positions as coaches. Our study team focused on the evolving roles within the school–university partnership because, as the roles were changing, the group of site coordinator or instructional coaches and site professors decided that they needed to have conversations to clearly understand the process and the impact on the district. These dialogs began as way to understand how combining the roles would change the work in the district and in the PDSs and how the roles and responsibilities would evolve as a way to support the culture of each PDS.

The four schools involved in the school–university partnership made a concerted effort to maximize this time to study the roles of instructional coaches, site coordinators, and site professors as each role was constantly evolving, as those job descriptions changed, and as needs at our individual schools changed. The focus question for our group became, How can the evolving roles of the site coordinator or instructional coach for site professors in the current school–university partnership schools support student learning through the four functions of a school–university partnership? To answer the question regarding our evolving roles, we needed to document and collect evidence about our roles and what the impact of these roles was and could be.

The evidence we collected came from several individuals involved in the school–university partnership. Our study group participated in a critical analysis of texts related to each role. These discussions were recorded and transcribed. Additionally, we interviewed each other over the course of the academic year. All of these discussions were audiotaped and transcribed. We looked for themes within those transcriptions. We also conducted interviews and surveys with teacher candidates, clinical teachers, and K–12 students at each of our PDSs and conducted a theme analysis of those results. These three perspectives of data or information provided us a foundation for describing and analyzing our roles in relation to the four partnership functions and the impacts of those roles on student learning. The process of our data collection and the results of the analysis of that data led to implications beyond the work we do in our individual PDSs. In the next sections, we describe how the conversations that began in our study group have given us a foundation for continuing to work together to look at how the partnership could support teacher education, teacher induction, and teacher retention throughout the entire school district.

Results and Impact

Data from the three perspectives reflect the importance of building internal capital in the form of relationships. Through these relationships, the evolution of roles became more purposeful. Change is inevitable, yet how individuals respond to and perceive change is critical. The insights gathered from various perspectives highlighted the evolution of the job roles, the impact on student learning, and the support for coteaching.

From one of our study group dialogues, the site coordinator or instructional coach reacted to an article we read with regards to evolving:

> There's a paragraph that talks about since the inception of the program the site coordinator position description and the position

itself have evolved and that verb, to me, just jumped right out, because I think that is what we're doing also. So is everybody else in the partnership. Everyone is evolving, but it is always evolving.

Clearly, the development of roles was centered around student learning on different levels. At the school level, we realized that relationships were key to the position—collaborative relationships with all teachers in the building. Where a site coordinator may interact primarily with teachers who are clinical teachers, an instructional coach is responsible for all teachers. So as the roles emerged, we found that collaborative relationships with all teachers enhanced the partnership because in this new role, the instructional coach/site coordinator knew about and could communicate with others about the partnership and utilize the resources of the partnership across all teachers in the school, not just clinical teachers who worked with teacher candidates. The coaching relationship with teacher candidates and all teachers in the building placed more emphasis on distributing leadership to clinical teachers to take a larger role in coaching teacher candidates, as well as less experienced peers.

The third type of relationship was the coteaching relationship. Coteaching offers another opportunity to build relationships right in front of the K–12 students. Because a variety of configurations can be involved in coteaching, teachers can utilize the process to enrich the teaching experience for the students as well as themselves. Coteaching is encouraged in many combinations among teacher candidates, site coordinators, site professors, clinical teachers, special education teachers, and other staff throughout the building. It is not unusual that a teacher candidate takes over an entire class so that two experienced teachers can coteacher together.

Linking to Internal Capital

When we combined the job descriptions and roles of the site coordinator and instructional coach and discussed the two positions through the forum of the study group, it became evident that the two discrete jobs were similar. Through collecting data on the impact of these roles in the schools, we discovered that this role relationship could build the internal capital of PDSs in school districts. The entire school clearly recognized that by having the site coordinator in the role of instructional coach, this role became one of a school leader; the instructional coach/site coordinator was seen working with veteran teachers as well as preservice teachers. Because the PDS faculty recognized the title of instructional coach, they were more willing to seek out consultation from this individual. In turn, this led to the refinement of practice and strengthened the functions of the partnership by all of the teachers (preservice and in-service) involved.

Because we knew that as we tried out our "new" job descriptions, our roles would evolve and we would be creating a model that could potentially be used elsewhere, we thought it was important to document our experience. We also hold at the center of all our work student learning, and we wanted to clearly articulate how our roles support a collaborative effort for positive impacts on students in the classrooms of these four schools. What we didn't know when we began this journey was that the roles of instructional coach and site coordinator could be so seamlessly joined. Nor did we realize the impact that our group could have on the policies of the entire district in relation to preservice teacher education, teacher induction, and teacher retention.

Continuing the Conversations

Throughout the next year, the school district PDS team continued meeting with district-level administrators. In summary, the meetings covered a variety of issues: funding, staffing, and job descriptions. Even though the PDS literature supports a trend that preservice teachers who train in the PDS model have a higher retention rate and the retention rate has been noted to be higher in this specific district, funding the roles within the PDS was a challenge. Continually, the issue was raised as to why the district was not funding the PDS if they were in full support of the concept. While they were supportive of the philosophical underpinnings of the PDS, the financial constraints and the lack of data supporting direct correlation to student learning impeded full fiscal funding. The team investigated a variety of sources, including private foundations and corporations. Since this school district currently is the largest school district in the state and has the highest teacher retention rate in the state, we were able to gain support from one foundation that seemed to understand our fiscal needs and vision.

The school district has a high level of commitment for increasing student performance and closing existing achievement gaps in the areas of race, ethnicity, and gender. The superintendent and board of education have set high expectations for all stakeholders to focus on accomplishing this work. As we examine supporting all teachers to be high performing, one area that we feel needs emphasis is the development of teachers from preservice through their first 3 to 5 years in a classroom. Currently, we have grown the partnership with the university to five of the district's schools. This partnership enables a preservice teacher to spend all preservice training time in one school with the support of a university site professor who works with the preservice teachers (teacher candidates) in classrooms and at the school site as well as teaching university classes. It also includes an instructional coach/site coordinator who is a master teacher working with both the clinical teacher (classroom teacher) and the teacher candidate, providing day-to-day support for both. Coteaching supports a way to close the achievement gap, increase student scores, and build relationships that create a cohesive school community. Also essential to this model is a principal who leads a school dedicated to collaboration and establishes a culture that supports ongoing, site-based, job-embedded teacher learning at all levels.

Through a systems change approach, the district and the university have collaboratively redefined the roles and responsibilities of the partnership personnel. This retuning has resulted in an intangible asset. Those assets give support to PDSs across a district. The deepening of the relationships and the continual redefinition of the evolving roles has supported the district so well that it has decided to implement policy changes and financial commitments. Systematically, these changes will and do link teacher education with recruitment, induction, and retention. These tangible assets become visible not only to the members in the partnership but also to members outside the partnership. Ideally, communities will start to ask for PDSs in their communities, turning the intangible into the tangible.

Acknowledgments

Special thanks for the dialog and insights from Judy Heinz, Carol Kaiser, Paula Lindenberger, Flo Olson, Robin Techmanski, and Stephanie Townsend. In addition, acknowledgment is given to Carole Basile, Sue Gill, and Chrysann McBride for their leadership and insight.

The Impact of Internal Capital

Systems that operate the partnership decision-making process are a critical piece of capital that should not be underestimated. It was the building of systems in each of this chapter's stories that allowed external capital, such as community practice and district involvement in partnership roles and responsibilities, and human capital, such as professional learning of technology, assessment, or coteaching, to exist. It was the systems that were put in place that allowed work to be accomplished in a manner that, in every case, was cohesive and collaborative.

These are the systems that allow for implementation of activity that is organized, efficient, and logical. It provides the data for accountability as these activities are communicated with the external community. And, it is the feedback from these systems that informs and educates the people involved to ensure that students are the ultimate beneficiaries.

Chapter 6

Building Human Capital
Creating Lifelong Learners

Human capital—that's what schools are all about—people. Educators are continuously looking for new instructional strategies, curricula, and methods of assessment so that they can develop their skills and knowledge through professional learning. The primary themes in building human capital include relationships, collaboration, and professional learning.

First, in a study of our program, over 321 photographs were taken by site professors and site coordinators in answer to the question "How does the partnership impact student learning?" A description of each photo was written and then analyzed for thematic congruence. Out of all of the pictures that were taken, 84% were taken because they illustrated a relationship that the photographer believed impacted student learning (i.e., teacher candidates and students, teacher candidates and clinical teachers, groups of teachers in professional learning cadres, principals with site professors and site coordinators). This illustrated the power that relationships can have on teaching and student learning and how doors are opened in a PDS and isolation can become a thing of the past.

Second, building human capital is about building collaboration. As one clinical teacher said, "As a result of the partnership, I learned to speak collaboratively." A principal stated,

Our site professor really helped me see that I needed to speak to teachers and to our site coordinator about their ideas. It took a year for me to get there, but I think my relationships are better and share information and ideas more...that's stopped teachers feeling so isolated.

And a site coordinator told us,

In our discussions this summer about the [new program], our school was done in an hour, while others (in other schools) labored for the

rest of the day. We get to consensus much faster since we've worked
as a partner school and built relationships throughout the building.

The collaborative spirit that is built through the partnership is crucial
to its success and ability to impact the culture of the school.

And finally, the third component is professional learning—professional
learning that comes from a variety of sources and configurations such as
teacher candidates bringing best practices to the classroom and asking
for evidence of learning, site coordinators and site professors supporting clinical teachers, inquiry and research, and external resources resulting
from grants and other university projects.

In this chapter, we'll see examples of school teams that are building
human capital in many ways. Some of the essays will reflect professional
learning of teachers through study groups embedded in the school day
and the development of a math culture that includes teachers and teacher
candidates. In other essays, we'll see a site professor who is working with
a group of high-risk youths, trying to impact student effort and motivation; a site coordinator who is preparing teachers to work with linguistically diverse students; and the impact of action research and inquiry as a
way to build reflective practitioners. In every case, we'll see how collaboration and relationships are built and how this impacts the school culture
and student learning.

A Middle School Study Group That Works

Kelli Varney and Rick VanDeWeghe

Intangible asset: "evidence that teachers are reflecting on instructional
practice as a result of the partnership"

The setting in this story is Racer Middle School, an inner-city school
with a large Hispanic student population and a dedicated staff and
administration. In 2001, a group of Racer clinical teachers, the site
coordinator, and the site professor sensed a tension between their
hard work in supporting and developing the university students who
intern at the school and their desire for professional development
and renewal. Starting in a brief, initial meeting where these concerns

were raised and discussed, these staff members embarked on a long journey that has had one primary goal—to create a study group that would inquire into their own teaching practices in order to better understand the teaching-learning enterprise.

It's a hot August day in the school cafeteria. Teachers wait anxiously to be dismissed from the morning staff meetings so they can prepare for the barrage of new students they expect in the next couple of days. Already feeling inundated by the amount of work that needs to be done before the first bell rings, they are struck by the principal's announcement: "Everyone *must* participate in action research during the school year," she proclaims proudly. Grumbling emerges from various parts of the room: "I'm not doing any more work for her," and "What the heck is action research?" The principal informs her staff that the results of their individual research projects will be directly tied to each staff member's yearly performance objectives. Everyone leaves the meeting feeling overwhelmed and unhappy.

Six years later at the same inner-city middle school, teachers are meeting in a more comfortable space, no longer on uncomfortable cafeteria benches. They are much happier, much more involved group of teachers sits down over lunch to discuss the results of a recent inquiry project conducted by one of their colleagues. Group members are excited to come together and share bits and pieces of what is happening in each other's classrooms. During the course of the meeting, a first-year teacher on staff pops his head in the door, disguising his entry by asking a teammate a question that could have waited—his real intent is to absorb part of the current discussion. One group member whispers to the facilitator, "He really wants to join our group, you know." Many of these teachers are the same as those who sat on the uncomfortable cafeteria benches years ago. The difference here has nothing to do with the physical space but rather the entire culture of the meeting. This meeting values and celebrates the expertise of these teachers. Members have the opportunity to share with others what they've learned about their students and how that knowledge is changing how they teach. Together, they have formed a unique bond, one that respects the differences they all bring and disclose. Most importantly, though, this has all developed from the bottom up. No one is making them attend, they are not being graded on anything they do or don't do during their time together, and participation is strictly voluntary. How this second scenario came about is a story of professional development in an urban middle school. It is a story of teacher initiative and leadership, classroom inquiry, collaboration, school–university partnership, reflective practice, and demonstrable commitment to not repeat the mistakes of the past that led to the first scenario.

While study groups are fairly common in U.S. schools and in university–school partnerships, what makes this professional development project unique may be that it successfully blends school–university partnership, site-based leadership and expertise, action research, and federal initiatives (e.g., No Child Left Behind) to improve teacher quality. It is also unique in that, from the start, participation has been voluntary yet has doubled in 3 years to become nearly one-fourth of the school staff. Further, contrary to many professional development projects that are discipline specific, this is interdisciplinary. As one teacher said recently, "It's more about being a better teacher than being a better math, science, etc., teacher." Finally, there is no fixed ending to the project, as in a credit-bearing university course, which allows the direction of the group to shift as group interests, questions, and wonderings shift. This successful experiment in professional development has teacher research at its center, a core guided by a number of principles and best practices associated with successful school-based professional development.

Principles

Inquiry

As a professional development school (PDS), we had a good record of promoting the professional development of teacher candidates, but less so for clinical teachers, because so much of our energy had been going into preparing those teacher candidates. Further, some of us knew, either intuitively or cognitively, that we needed to connect inquiry with practice in intellectually compelling ways in order for Racer to be considered a PDS for *all* its learners—students, teacher candidates, clinical teachers, site coordinator, and site professor.

Inquiry, rather than action research, seemed an attractive idea to many of the teachers who harbored bad memories of the previous attempt at large-scale professional development through imposed action research. We also knew that the school–university partnership presented a unique opportunity to draw on a wealth of resources, at the center of which are those teachers at the school. Though we didn't realize then as we do now, we were developing into a genuine learning community with site-based expertise and with inquiry directed at our own teaching practices.

In top-down models, perceived expertise comes from outside, such as university faculty or professional consultants. Top-down models are often less effective because the motivation to complete a given task doesn't come from the individual completing it. What we believed, however, was that expertise lies within—among our seasoned teachers as well as among our new teachers, all of whom brought to the project inquiring minds that said, "Yes, I'd like to know more about good teaching, and yes, I might have some good ideas on that topic that I can share."

In addition, since we knew we sought more understanding into the efficacy of teaching practices in order to better understand student learning and achievement, we encouraged and supported one another in reflective practice.

Evolution

Our initial endeavors were guided by what we knew through experience about how professional development can easily fail, as seen earlier in this essay, and by what we knew through review of professional development sources about how it can succeed. The history of failure was a simple one. Years ago, a former administrator, in conjunction with the university, had determined that action research would be implemented at the school, and not only the clinical teachers in the Initial Professional Teacher Education (IPTE) program but the entire staff would design and put into place classroom research projects. There was no choice in the matter, it was simply a mandate. Some of us vividly remembered this well-intentioned but ill-conceived attempt to promote professional development: we remembered the hostility it generated, we rehashed the frustrations we felt over a lack of understanding about inquiry, and we recalled the resistance, primarily passive but also outright. The project went absolutely nowhere.

In contrast, our study group began with only a rudimentary understanding of inquiry and little previous recognition that the teachers themselves were rich sources of expertise but with an inclination to engage in reflective practice. All of these dimensions evolved over time, and continue to evolve, with every teacher located somewhere on a spectrum of professional development. Some are more advanced than others in some ways (e.g., collecting data), while others are more proficient in other ways (e.g., asking good questions). But, because this is a learning community, we do not expect everyone to be at the same place on the spectrum. That is the democratic principle clearly at work here—everyone is learning and developing as we continue our work.

Perhaps the best metaphor for the evolution of this group may be the Mississippi River, which has been known to change its course due to natural forces. So, too, the study group has shifted its course as it has evolved. Indeed, change has become crucial to the longevity of the group because such flexibility has allowed us to follow the shifting interests and needs of the members over time.

The study group was born out of discomfort. That is, our clinical teachers felt that, although they were strongly supportive of the teacher candidates with whom they worked, they, on the other hand, were lacking in their own professional development during the school day. Following discussion about what they might want in the way of professional development, we settled upon pursuit of one thing that all teachers have in common, and that is *classroom talk*. In its broadest sense, "talk" is the linguistic sea upon which most instruction floats; it is one of the most essential and common vehicles by which teachers from all disciplines teach; and it quickly became apparent that it is a phenomenon that few, if any teachers had ever seriously considered. Thus, classroom talk became an issue that we hoped to illuminate over time and the launching point for the work of the study group.

At an initial meeting, we collaborated on a speculative taxonomy of classroom talk, brainstorming and listing the multiple ways in which talk figures in the daily life of the classroom. Teacher talk, student talk, questioning, responding, body language, nonverbal linguistic cues, and so on, became our broad guideposts, each of which, over time, was broken down into parts as the group continued to analyze and refine the taxonomy. We then narrowed our focus to *teacher talk* and decided to seek understanding of the types of teacher talk, the frequency of those types, and what research on teacher talk reveals about the relative effectiveness of teacher talk in learning. We anticipated that at a later point we might investigate student talk as well.

We agreed to videotape individual teachers working with whole classes, bring those tapes to our monthly meetings, and view them with the goal of gaining greater understanding into teacher talk. At first, there was great trepidation among these teachers, not only toward having themselves videotaped but also toward allowing colleagues to see the tapes. Though five teachers immediately volunteered to have themselves videotaped, others worried that they would be evaluated when the group watched the tapes. However, as the goal of understanding, not evaluating, classroom talk became the group ethos, such fears began to dissipate because we viewed the tapes as "data" that would illuminate further our growing understanding of teacher talk. In keeping with this group ethos, data was understood as something we could learn from, not something we would judge—a habit of mind that was crucial to establishing a sense of safety among the group members at the time.

We decided that all meetings would take place during the school day, not after school. In order to make time for meetings, the teacher candidates became responsible for their clinical teachers' class or duty coverage. This arrangement benefited both groups: the clinical teachers gained a crucial uninterrupted block of time for their professional development in a collegial setting, and the teacher candidates gained more time working with whole classes without their clinical teachers' presence in the room. When the principal agreed to provide lunch for our meetings, we not only gained demonstrable support from the administration, but we also enacted our firm belief that food enhances mood.

For the first year, then, we viewed tapes, developed our understanding of teacher talk, and refined the taxonomy. Our readings on classroom talk gave descriptive language to some of the ways we were coming to understand the relationships between classroom talk and student achievement. For example, research on dialogic classrooms (Nystrand, Wu, Gamoran, Zeiser, & Long, 2003) helped us to see how teachers' responses to students' talk (viz., "uptake") can affect achievement. Similarly, research into how teachers' talk with students about "intelligence" has direct bearing on students' academic success illuminated our understanding of teacher praise (Dweck, 2002).

Discussions spurred by the videotape viewings and the reading moved individual teachers to wonder about talk in their respective classrooms. For example, in our discussion of authentic versus inauthentic questions, one teacher wondered if the Colorado Student Academic Profile (CSAP) annual tests mainly encouraged low-level, inauthentic questions, while another speculated that in science, students may be encouraged to exercise low-level thinking because, in part, the textbooks are written such that they do not encourage higher-level thinking.

These kinds of wonderings marked this phase in our process of inquiry and led into the next phase (year 2) of the study group, one that moved us naturally toward more habits of mind associated with teacher research—speculation and empiricism. We began discussing conducting informal "tiny experiments" in which teachers, alone or in collaboration, would seek understanding of a speculative question about teacher talk by gathering data. To ward off negative associations teachers had with action research, we used the term "tiny experiments," by which we meant the following:

- Teachers would ask "What happens?" questions, such as, "What happens when we focus more on speculation and imagination in our own questions directed toward students?"
- Teachers would try to have a narrow focus, such as, "What is the ratio of authentic to inauthentic questions in my classroom?"

- Teachers would gather data that illuminated understanding of the questions through such means as sociograms, surveys, and observations.
- Teachers would report back to the group on what they learned from their experiments.

A few teachers quickly committed to conducting an experiment. One teacher worked with active questioning strategies, such as "I understand _____, but what I don't understand is _____"; another looked into working with his teacher candidate to encourage students to read using question-answer-relationship questions, (where the answer is "right there in the text," "between the lines," or "beyond the text"). But while every teacher agreed to conduct an experiment, actually doing so was slow going—some had trouble finding a focus, and energy dropped considerably as the end of the school year approached.

Then came summer vacation, and nothing except *thinking* about classroom talk transpired until school resumed in August. However, during this time, the site coordinator and site professor, through the university, secured a small grant to support the study group during the next year. With the grant money, we were able to provide small stipends to teachers and light lunches for our meetings. While having stipends and food was "nice," as one person put it, membership remained voluntary, because it was the community that now mattered most, a collaborative body that wanted to continue its work for the sheer intellectual and social benefits. We thus began the school year as a true learning community—in it for the learning, period.

We began our third year with an agenda that had been set in the spring—to conduct tiny experiments. We set our meeting agendas one month in advance, asking for volunteers each time to report on their experiments. Slowly, some teachers volunteered to present, while others held back, often commenting that they could not find a focus, could not decide what data to collect, and, most commonly, did not have the time to experiment. Nonetheless, enough did volunteer to get us more involved in the processes of classroom research. One math teacher shared with us the results of her experiment—a student survey that investigated her students' views of their intelligence. After analyzing her data, she was disturbed to discover that one of her classes had a large percentage of students who believed that their intelligence is "fixed" (either you have it or you don't); she decided therefore to continue with the experiment by using more "process praise" (Dweck, 2002) to see if that percentage would change over time.

When another teacher investigated her students' perceptions of what makes a "good" teacher, a "bad" teacher, and "good" and "bad" students, we used our meeting time to analyze her data (student surveys) collaboratively. This was a crucial meeting, for in the process of analyzing the data (noticing patterns, another habit of mind), most of the group members experienced for the first time what it means to collect and analyze data, which together constitute another habit of mind we might call empiricism. For many in the group, it became apparent that data collection can be undertaken without great statistical machinery, can be analyzed easily, and, most important, can be a source of learning that will inform instruction and affect achievement.

Present Structures and Struggles

Presently the study group meets formally on a monthly basis. Meetings are scheduled during the school hours, and lunch is served at each of the meetings. Class coverage is provided for any participant who needs it. The teacher candidates in the building are who provide the class coverage during these period long meetings. Except for one new member, the group has remained very stable for the past 2 years.

The group as a whole still has struggles. Without concrete examples, many of the members have trouble formulating good survey questions that could provide interesting feedback from students. After collecting data in a classroom, we've found that we don't naturally know what to do with it. So, the group has decided to take time to look at how to analyze data in a meaningful way. The idea that data has distinct patterns was not apparent to all group members from the beginning. Looking at authentic data gathered by group members has helped with this process. Although the study group has also begun to understand that these processes take an immense amount of time, time is the one resource we could use more of. Because the partnership exists at Racer, the teacher candidates can be utilized for class coverage during the school day meetings. However, the study group members have found it necessary to spend some quality time other than during their workday to take a good long look at any data they collect. The site coordinator has been involved on occasion to cover class for a study group member, collect data during class time and synthesize data submitted by group members.

We expect that struggles such as these (and others yet to be encountered) will continue as a natural part of the evolution of the study group. As coordinators of the group, we see such challenges as opportunities for our own professional development as members of this learning community. Not only are we learning more about teacher talk and action research, but we are also learning about the continuum of professional development and how teachers' engagement may be viewed and valued in different ways. To illustrate, we present below three teachers' experiences in the study group that we feel represent teachers at different points of engagement. Each person is truly engaged with the group, though the forms of engagement differ.

Lee, an experienced science teacher, describes his engagement with the group as "reserved," by which he means quiet listening and subsequent application of his learning to his teaching and his mentoring of his teacher candidate: "I gain most by listening and taking ideas back to the classroom." Lee's form of engagement is reflective; at times he says, "I feel an impulse to contribute what I think might be helpful [but then] I just let the discussion continue." Early on, and at the nudging of another teacher, Lee took on a leadership role by having himself videotaped for the group during a class session when he and his students engaged in storytelling. "This tape put me in a modeling role for the study group," he reported. Still, his primary form of engaging with the work of the group continues to be an unassuming one: "I will continue to sit back and take in the sharing of ideas that contribute to my duties as a clinical teacher and as a classroom teacher."

Annie, another science teacher (in her fourth year), is ordinarily an outspoken staff member, yet she has deliberately striven to learn "more as a sponge than a barracuda!" Being one who finds "listening by not talking a difficult challenge," she has discovered that she "likes her role and [is] moving toward understanding that listening can be as much a contribution as talking." In our meetings, we often see her struggling to withhold opinion as she can become visibly excited by the exchange of ideas and opinions. In her words, "In the group, as one person is speaking, I'm often forming ideas of how to respond…rather than really hearing what the person is saying." Annie's public silence may appear on the surface as not terribly engaged, yet when she approaches the group coordinator after a meeting to say, privately, "This is so fantastic!" there is no doubt that her form of engagement, though out of character, is profound: "My thoughts and reflections are a valuable tool as I move to implement some of the skills I am hearing about."

Tami, a first-year literacy teacher and a recent member of the group, seems to blend the reflective engagement typical of Lee and the normally verbally active nature of Annie with her own natural curiosity about teaching and learning, as well as with her penchant for gathering and learning from data. In the group, Tami quickly developed an inquiry project—noticing that "some students volunteer to share all the time in class while others silently hope to become invisible," she developed a survey that invited students to give insight into their perceptions of their roles as learners in her classes. The survey results stimulated more curiosity as she then began wondering about what messages she conveys regarding in-class discussion and what her students think about the value of their own voices: "Do they feel like I think their voice is important?" "Do they think they have to be right in order to speak?" "If I do not show value for their voice, why should they?" Armed with this more elaborate set of questions, Tami began a close analysis of the results of her survey with the goal of connecting her assessment with her instruction: "Hopefully, I will learn from the data and be able to experiment with my teaching to affect change in my thinking and in the actions/ participation of my students."

Three teachers, three forms of engagement, all on a spectrum of professional development, none more—or less—engaged than the others, each different from the others, and each making important contributions to the success of the group: their various forms of engagement have reinforced for us the most important perspective we can bring to our own classrooms, and that is to notice each learner carefully, to value the diverse ways they do learn, and to recognize that individual differences of these sorts make the ethos of the group (and our classrooms) truly supportive of learning.

What We Have Learned About Building Human Capital

Our experience thus far has reaffirmed the essential principles of professional development upon which the project is based, as stated at the start of this essay: inquiry that would illuminate and improve instruction, recognition of on-site expertise, and frequent opportunities for reflective practice. We have also learned a number of other things that we now consider essential to a site-based project such as this:

- *Collaboration is crucial.* Clinical teachers, teacher candidates, site coordinators, faculty, and administrators working together to establish and maintain a genuine learning community.
- *Teachers want to be learners too.* Teachers have a natural inclination and strong professional sense of obligation to learn more about teaching and learning; they want to be learners along with their students and their teacher candidates.
- *Time matters.* Successful professional development takes time; time to meet without interruption, time to observe and learn from students, and time to reflect upon practice.

- *Data is transformative*: Examining data that challenges teachers' ways of thinking about practice, good teachers are impelled to change.
- *Understanding must be the goal.* Many problems are complex and do not lend themselves to quick fixes. They call for understanding first before solutions can be considered.
- *Professional development is a continuum.* Differentiating professional development helped us recognize and value each teacher and the important role they play in the process of change.
- *Voluntary participation creates a genuine community.* When each person is there on their own volition and with an authentic reason for continuing with the group, the group learns.
- *Fostering the habits of mind associated with action research has lasting effects.* These skills nurture teaching based on data not false assumptions.

Link to Building Human Capital

The Racer Middle School Study Group represents the paradigm shift in professional development called for by experts for nearly a decade (Sparks & Hirsch, 1997). It is a shift from large-scale reform to reform brought about by small learning communities (Schmoker, 2004). And while we at Racer may not know where the next change in the course of the river may take us, we have come to value that change and trust that it will lead us into yet more opportunities for continued learning and growth. However, we also firmly believe that without the partnership's focus on human capital, this school would not have embarked on such a project that is making a difference for teachers and students.

Ready for Life, Ready for School

Oscar Joseph III

Intangible asset: "utilization of site coordinators' and site professors' direct impact on student learning"

Sage Middle School is in the heart of Denver, a neighborhood school offering students a challenging curriculum that meets a variety of students' needs in both academic and extracurricular programs. The faculty at Sage has a strong commitment to the community, providing an academically challenging environment. Students at Sage are predominantly African American (76%) and Hispanic (17%). Sage has recently developed a school-within-a-school model with three academies that address the different needs of students. The site professor at Sage has engaged boys in a program to build self-confidence and student achievement. These students were identified as having high socioemotional and academic needs.

At 7:30 a.m., I arrived at the school. The first thing I needed to do was order pizza for 15 young men, primarily African American, 12 years of age, a group of students with a high number of detentions, referrals, and behavior problems, all referred to me by counselors, the special education teacher, and an administrator. We had met and talked about the kind of pizza and drinks they wanted, so I had a tall order to fill. I had bought sport drinks on my way to school, so now it was just the pizza.

Fifth period approached, and I needed to gather the students from the lunchroom. Amid all the chatter and conversation, I found the young men I was looking for and gathered the students in the northeast corner of the cafeteria. They had all given up recess, a most precious time of the day, to participate in this program. I told them about myself, gave out the drinks, and provided them with our first agenda item, moving from the cafeteria to the meeting room.

As we moved through the hall, the administrators could not believe their positive hallway behavior. The lunchroom was on the second floor, the meeting room was on the first floor, so it took us a while to get to the room. It was the beginning of a longer journey than I had thought possible. This was the beginning of a program called Striving for Academic Greatness and Excellence (SAGE).

The Journey Begins

The room we were assigned was a "community classroom." I had the pizza, writing paper, and pencils ready for them. But before we entered the room, I told them "Coming into this classroom is a not a right, it's a privilege" and then took them, one at a time into the room. After they were in their seats, the first thing I did was to put my football helmet on the table and talk about being a student athlete. I talked about the insignia on the helmet and how few people get to wear the purple and white of Northwestern University. I talked about how it was a privilege not a right to be an alumnus of this university. I showed them the decals that covered the helmet, awards for a great play, a touchdown, or an important tackle. I told them that this was analogous to doing things well in school, a great paper, appropriate behavior...but not everyone gets these decals, you have to earn them. You earn your grades, you earn the right to progress to high school, and you earn the right to graduate. The helmet is a symbol of my affiliation to a larger community. I told them that they are a group of young men for whom excellence is the only option: "That is the standard, and that's what we'll achieve." At that point, some kids asked, "How long are we going to do this?" "Next week?" "The semester?" "All year?" I told them once a week all year. I got a lot of "YES, OH YEAH!"

So off we went. I talked to them about my middle school years and asked them about how their middle school days were going. I told them that the agenda for our time together was to develop their life missions, and with curiosity and eagerness they left the first session.

Beginning With the End in Mind

The first session was to connect their academic content with their cultural life. A lot of the kids talked about wanting to be an athlete. I told them I was an athlete, but athletics doesn't last forever. "What do you think a life mission is?" Students said, "It's something that you might do, a plan for the future." I told them they were absolutely right, they needed to have vision: "Why are you here? What are you doing here at this middle school?" I used the term *vision* because I felt it was a constant; a *dream* could fade away. Every student had to write his life mission and was asked to present it to the group. When a student stood to present, the other students were asked to applaud him for his effort, for his thoughts, and to show him respect. What was interesting was how their peers began to connect with what he wanted to do. We had students who wanted to be doctors or realtors or run janitorial businesses. They had some idea about what they wanted to do but didn't know how to get there.

The following sessions included leadership and entrepreneurship. Students were elected by their peers to be captains, senators, or community activists. And the program is still going on. We're taking field trips, like touching the turf at Mile High Stadium and going to the Nature and Science Museum, the Colorado History Museum, and music studios. I want to introduce them to their future mirrors, people of color who have already become what they want to become. These are the things these students need to be exposed to in order to become what they foresee. They need to get ready for life so that they can be ready for school.

Class or Support Group

This isn't a support group; this is a rigorous, academic class that supports students just like any other class supports students. It's a class that integrates writing, reading, and speaking. It makes connections with the social sciences, music, and art. When I asked students who influences them, no one could answer. Pizza got them there, but it's the connections that keep them there. Yes, I'm African American, but is it my ethnicity that keeps them coming? No, it's that students have found genuineness, someone who cares, and someone they can relate to.

One student was in another class, and the teacher commented to him that his behavior was not appropriate: she knew he was in Dr. J's class and this wasn't what he would expect. The student responded that he was only in it for the pizza, which we still have every week. When the student came to the next class, he was told that he couldn't stay—it's a privilege to join the group, not a right. The others in the class applauded and agreed that this student couldn't be in the group that day. Sure, other kids were probably in the group for the pizza at first, but they aren't now. When two young men were suspended for fighting, the rest of the group wanted to know if they were out of the group. I said no, because everyone makes mistakes, and we have to learn how to fix those mistakes. You have to learn from your failure to grow. The students were amazed; this was different. It all sounds a bit like preaching, but the fact is this intervention has impact because they know there is someone who cares.

Baby Steps

One day, one of the students was walking out the door of his math classroom with a chair. (He had gotten in trouble and had been asked to take his chair out to the hallway and sit.) As he saw me coming, he started walking the other way down the hall, but of course he couldn't go far. As I approached, his head bent down so that his chin was on his chest. I reminded him that he had just been chosen captain of the group; how could he lead if he was in the hallway.

"If you were in business you would have lost your $500 bonus. What have you learned today?"

"Nothing."

"Right. What have you earned today?"

"Nothing."

"Right."

Everything is a learning process. Everything must be interconnected and can be used as a teaching experience. Teach the child that this is not where he wants to be and every behavior impacts his day, his year, and his life. As educators, we need to pay attention to teachable moments and look for them so students can learn from their mistakes, not wallow in them.

Teachers are coming to me about student performance. Students are encouraged to respect teachers and other adults, learn proper etiquette, and behave in a manner that allows them to move forward in life. "Education is...knowledge for my life." This is the cadence that these students have learned in the classroom, but they say it in the hallway, out in public, in their church, and with their families. They need to think about their education as that which will help them with their lives. Knowledge needs to be real, contextual, and authentic. Episodic and routine facts don't take care of families. Taking care of families means that they need a meaningful, well-rounded education that addresses their personal, social, and academic needs.

Link to Building Human Capital

Who am I? I'm not a teacher in the school, not the guidance counselor, not a school administrator. I'm a university professor who spends time in the school because this is a professional development school, where everyone is a student and everyone is there to help kids in any way possible. The greatest human capital we have is our children, and I see it as my responsibility to work with students as well as teachers and teacher candidates to build human capital in the school.

Native Language to English:
A Transition for Everyone

Maria Uribe

Intangible asset: "utilization of teacher candidates' direct impact on student learning"

Every year, Garden Elementary's population varies from 630 to 650 students. Out of those 650 students, 350 have been identified from the English Language Acquisition Department (ELA) as English language learners (ELL). Every year, we have approximately 145 students who are new to our school and are recent immigrants from Mexico, Salvador, China, Cambodia, and Vietnam. Approximately 97 students have been in the United States for 2 years, and 135 students have been in the United States for 3 or 4 years. Every classroom has some ELL students due to the large number of students who speak another language other than English. Therefore, the entire staff has been trained or is getting trained to meet the ELL students' needs

Ten years ago, we became a professional development school. Teacher candidates came to our school because they had chosen the school or the university had assigned them. As teacher candidates came to the school, they realized very quickly that they were facing a different population of students than they had grown up with and they needed to change their vision and be prepared to work with linguistically diverse students. They needed to understand their own importance in the school and in classrooms as students were transitioning from their native language to English. Getting the teacher candidates to clarify what matters most, in what balance, with what trade-offs, became my central task (Heifetz, 1994).

Transition Players

There are a number of transition players in schools, including the clinical teachers, teacher candidates, university professors, students, parents, the community, the school administration, the site coordinator, and the site professor. All of them are involved in creating an environment that is conducive to student transition and learning.

Clinical teachers are teachers who have teacher candidates in their classroom. These teachers play a very important role because they have the responsibility to help the teacher candidate, but at the same time, they need to make sure that the children are also benefiting from the teacher candidates' instruction. Clinical teachers like to have teacher candidates because they have the opportunity to have another adult in the classroom who can help the students in a variety of ways (e.g., small group instruction, one-to-one reading, assessments). The clinical teachers are trained to teach second language learners. Some of them have English as second language endorsement, and some have completed the district training and have more than 3 years of experience with second language learners. They can provide the teacher candidates with a great amount of support for the challenge they have with second language learners. They were also aware of the lack of experience with linguistically diverse students the teacher candidates had and their need for training.

Teacher candidates came to the partnership schools to do their internships, which helped them to meet their university requirements, as well as to have the opportunity to gain experience in the field while they did their courses. They were the most important parts of the solution to my problem. Teacher candidates had to learn, understand, and apply their classroom techniques to fulfill students' needs, accommodating their instruction to the children that they were working with, and most of these candidates needed to work on their skills to teach and to relate with second language learners. Although the teacher candidates had to plan their instruction to meet the needs of all children, when they had second language learners, they had to arrange their plan to develop comprehension, vocabulary, and discussion.

The university professors and the school's site professor helped teacher candidates with the theory and the strategies that they could use in the classrooms. The professors needed to be more aware of the population that our school had to provide the teachers candidates more accurate information and strategies for the students to apply in their classroom. On campus they needed to provide an adaptive curriculum in which the teacher candidates could be prepared for the linguistically diverse students.

Parents were involved according to their own understanding culture and skills. Some of them visit classrooms, some of them work with their child at home, and some of them come for parent teacher conferences and make sure that they know their child's progress. However, some of them choose not to be involved with their child's learning because of legal issues. According to a parent survey completed in 2000, all of the parents want the best instruction for their children, and a strong majority of the parents are interested in their children's education.

Even though the students' academic performance varies, the students, in general, are willing to learn. The school has a balanced literacy program in which the students learn to work independently and in groups. The students' background knowledge varies: the school has both students that have been there since kindergarten and some who have not attended school for much time at all. Therefore, their skills in reading, writing, math, and other content areas are at different levels. The teachers have to plan and assess the children constantly to deliver instruction and meet the children's needs. From the moment the teacher candidates enter the classrooms, the children become part of their lives.

The school community is very interesting, with five very distinctive communities. We have the Hispanic, the Caucasian, the Asian, the African American, and the Native American communities. The children are very close to each other until they reach the upper grades. It is in the upper grades that the teachers start seeing cliques and racial discrimination between students occur. The coherence of the external community is very important if students are to get beyond these social boundaries and continue their learning.

Over the past 10 years, the school has had two principals. In each of their tenures they have supported the partnership with the university. They have delegated all the responsibility to the site professor and the site coordinator. They have participated in a monthly meeting with the university where all principals of PDSs have the opportunity to bring issues concerning the teacher preparation program. In addition, the assistant principal, whose role it is to delegate discipline functions, ensures that teacher candidates follow the correct procedures to deliver instruction and implement the discipline program she has put in place at Garden Elementary.

I am the site coordinator, constantly interacting with principal, assistant principal, clinical teachers, teachers, staff members, students, and parents. I have to be aware of the issues that come up with the teacher candidates (e.g., lessons, discipline, and professionalism). The site professor and I provide the environment the teacher candidates need to work with second language learners.

In the past 4 years, the site professor has changed three times; however, the goal of helping teacher candidates has always been their priority. The site professor is the connection between the school and the university. The site professor and the site coordinator work closely together to help teacher candidates with the issues they face in a multilingual school. The site professor is also responsible for communicating school issues to the university so that university faculty can modify or change the program to better serve the teacher candidates. The site professor has been a key player in my leadership plan; she ensures that I have time with teacher candidates to develop a better understanding of the importance of working with and for linguistically diverse students.

Teacher Candidates and Second Language Learners

Four years ago, I started to work as a site coordinator. My task has been to place teacher candidates in classrooms, guide them to adapt to the population they are working with, and make sure the school is providing a good experience during their three internships but at the same time demonstrate to the school district that having teacher candidates in the classroom helps student learning. This job has been a challenge; placing teacher candidates has not been easy because most of them request "English" classrooms. Since we don't have those classrooms, teacher candidates have had to work in classrooms with second language learners even if it is not their choice. Teacher candidates need to understand that schools are facing day by day more and more linguistically diverse students. As a result, some of the teacher candidates felt very uncomfortable in those classrooms. They thought that if they were not bilingual they should not be in those classrooms. The lack of command in linguistically diverse students' language creates a fear of working with them. Upon entering the program, teacher candidates did not realize the different strategies they could use in the classroom to deliver their instruction and understand their students' language.

Teacher candidates needed to be oriented so they could adapt to the environment in which they were working. I also knew that each teacher candidate would bring her or his own philosophy and own experience to the school. The view of working with a second language varied in many degrees with each individual teacher candidate. They had, like every other person, their own philosophies about second language learners and children with different backgrounds. Some of them did not want to work with them because of their own beliefs and others because they wanted to feel successful in their internship. Therefore the challenge was to create an environment in which they could share their own values and work in the reality of their lives at that moment to avoid conflict among people in the school community. I had to be very careful with these issues so the adaptation had to come from them and not from me.

Teacher candidates had to work hard to be able to understand, respect, and be part of the second language learners' lives. The environment they grew up in provided them a perspective of life that was very different from the one they were encountering. Analyzing and identifying what the students needed was going to be a difficult task for teacher candidates.

My goal was to see the teacher candidates change their attitude toward, instruction of, and opinions of second language learners. First, the candidates had to feel like they were part of the community. They were invited to every school event, including staff development. They were also asked to complete a "legacy" project for the community that in some way would connect them to the greater school community.

Second, I used an adaptive approach, which involves a great amount of communication, in order to build trusting and confidential relationships between the teacher candidates and myself. We discussed issues like Colorado Student Academic Profile (CSAP) for second language learners. We talked about the legacy project they would do with the community, the experience of working with parents and community members, the celebrations and the frustrations of the classroom, and the ideas that have worked for them that have made them very proud. In his journal, one teacher candidate wrote,

> Before I began working at Garden I had never stepped foot in a public school. My elementary, high school as well as my college experience mostly consisted of little if any diversity. The first day I went to work at Garden I thought I was going to change the world. I wanted to become a role model to the children I worked with and to help them read and write. I quickly discovered that having the mentality that one can save the world was not what my students needed from me. In return the students refused to connect or make a true connection with me. I felt as though I was a definite "outsider." At first I did not know how to react to their rejection, as I had never felt such feelings before. It became a challenge to get up in the morning to go to work to do something that I love. I knew I had to do something to change or else I would never make a connection with my students. Instead of trying to save the world I decided to become a friend. I knew that the children thought they had nothing in common with me but I used that to make the connections. I decided that the children could actually teach me just as much as I could teach each of my students. Having such an experience made me realize how difficult it is for anyone whether he or she be a second language learner or not to come into a new environment and make the connections necessary to have a meaningful experience. I will always take this experience with me through my teaching career.

The second approach I used was "technical solutions." These technical solutions reflected instructional strategies that made sense and were appropriate for second language learners. The technical solutions that I used were

- English as second language workshops, sheltered English work-shops, and differences between language and academic achieve-ment workshops;
- communication and coaching with the site coordinator and the site professor;
- providing planning time for teachers candidates with clinical teachers.

At the beginning of my journey, I sat back and let the teacher candidates express their opinions about a variety of issues such as language acquisition, working with minorities, and frustrations they had within the classroom. I also observed how the site professor worked with the teacher candidates, noting the strategies she used to coach them and to help them to go through their internships. Each teacher candidate had to plan lessons that needed to be coached. The coaching consisted of a three-way process: first they had a preconference, second an observation of the lesson, and third a postconference.

After I observed and coached many teacher candidates, I started to ask specific questions about the instruction for English language learn-ers. Some of the teacher candidates were not aware of all the implications that planning a lesson involved. The majority thought that if they wrote the lesson plan in great detail it was going to be successful. These ques-tions made the teacher candidates aware of the issues they needed to address in the classroom.

I started to see the transition in their thinking during the pre- and postconferences. They were asking a number of questions regarding the strategies they should use with their students. This demonstrated an awareness of the necessity to learn more about the strategies, not only to teach second language learners but for all students in general. Some of them started to work collaboratively with their peers and other clinical teachers to create an environment in which both teachers and students benefited from the partnership. The purpose for their teaching was clear; teacher candidates took collaborative responsibility for student learning.

Building Human Capital

My goal has always been to build human capital around issues of lin-guistically diverse populations and create teacher candidates that are stu-dent advocates who understand the importance of being teachers for all students. At the same time, I want to provide a positive experience for teacher candidates. I want them to see the need to know how to work with diverse students and to help them as future teachers.

My work as a site coordinator has been a new challenge in my life. I needed to learn not only how to work with teacher candidates but also how to work with people who needed a change. I believe I have helped them to create new images of work that, at first, teacher candidates thought would be very hard to achieve. What more could I ask for—in the beginning teacher candidates stated that they were frustrated, unsure of themselves because they did not understand the children's culture, worried about how to communicate, or apprehensive because of the neighborhood. Over time, these teacher candidates became confident and competent teachers of second language learners. The partnership and teacher candidates add a lot to our school. They help us all grow, learn, and keep reflecting about the students who are sitting in front of us and how we can help them transition to a new world.

Action Research Teams for Student Learning

Stephanie Townsend and Linda Rickert

Intangible asset: "evidence of inquiry or action research and how it supports accountability processes and best practices implementation"

Stillwater Elementary school opened its doors in 1996. Since its inception it has been a professional development school. Stillwater is a suburban school with approximately 535 students, 76% Caucasian, 17% Hispanic, 2% Black, 3% Asian, and 1% Native American. Sixteen percent of the students qualify for free or reduced lunch, and they have a mobility rate of 19%. Nine percent of the students are English as second language learners. Inquiry at Stillwater has been a focus from the beginning. The teachers believe in building human capital by being reflective practitioners. Over the years, the school has done individual inquiry projects and schoolwide projects.

Last year the schoolwide inquiry question was, "In what ways does the University of Colorado Denver (UCD) partnership influence student learning?" Some of the students were interviewed, and the staff provided feedback four times during the year. Findings showed that having another adult in the classroom helps students ask questions and receive prompt answers; teacher candidates who substitute in the building provide continuity for student learning, especially when they substitute in their internship classroom; teachers enjoy the openness of having people walking in and around the classroom because it helps them to not feel so isolated.

The inquiry at Stillwater was schoolwide. When the site professor learned that every grade level team had a learning goal, she suggested that the school might want to do action research on these learning goals. She met with the principal and the leadership team to express her idea and share a possible schoolwide plan. The Team agreed this was an excellent focus for the school. After that meeting, the site professor met with most of the learning teams to provide additional support.

At the April clinical teacher seminar, the inquiry process was discussed again. It was decided that three learning teams would present their inquiry at a faculty meeting. Teachers prepared and shared a one-page document or a brochure about their inquiry project. The first learning team included two second grade teachers who wondered how to improve the conventions or mechanics their students use when they write (i.e., capitalization, subject and verb agreement, spelling, etc.). Their data sources included student writing samples, monthly assessment, writing to the same prompt, a score-embedded writing rubric, and looking at writing samples as a team. These teachers were given a district writing rubric to use when they assess students' writing, which they used along with student work to guide their writing instruction. The teachers also solicited help from the parents to improve the children's writing, especially in the area of conventions. As the teachers worked with their students, they realized that when they demonstrated writing lessons that connected to the second graders' real life, the students were more engaged and eager to edit the conventions that they used in their writing. Use of conventions improved during these lessons. However, the teachers were frustrated with the writing rubric because the district changed the rubric midyear, and when these teachers received the end-of-year rubric, it was different from the first. Once the teachers realized that they needed to focus on student work and not a rubric, they began to see areas of student growth and areas in which students still need more explicit instruction. Although this grade level had many personnel changes on their learning team this year, they persevered. The remaining team member wants to continue this action research next year.

The second learning team presentation of inquiry involved the special education teachers in the school. Members included the building psychologist, speech pathologists, early childhood specialist, and the resource room teacher. The team wanted to increase the number of special education students who achieved 80% or better on their individual goals and objectives. The team implemented reader–writer workshops, consulted and worked with classroom teachers, facilitated the second-to-third grade transition, shared physical space with each other on the team, and participated in collaborative teaching. The team achieved their goal. The presenter indicated that an additional benefit of this action research was the collaborative effort from each team member. The team had not worked in this manner before this inquiry. In the future, they intend to continue their collaborative working relationship to enhance the learning of their special needs students.

The third learning team involved two kindergarten teachers. One of the teachers has been trained in a district-sponsored early childhood math program and philosophy. The other teacher has not received the math training. These teachers wanted to track student math progress throughout the school year. They completed screening on every kindergarten student and conducted a math interview to assess student understanding, recorded progress on an individual math continuum monthly, and shared student samples and anecdotal notes to track students. These teachers noted that their goal was to keep track of student learning in math, and they were able to do this successfully.

The teachers found both groups of kindergarten students improved in mathematics understanding and achievement. Ninety percent of each kindergarten class achieved proficiency on the Jeffco Kindergarten Math Benchmarks. The teacher who was trained in the district's mathematics pilot program and the teacher who was not trained in the district's program used the same curricular materials. The trained teacher followed a scope and sequence for the curriculum that included scripted text to follow with each lesson. She also was required to reflect on each lesson to provide information for the creators of the program. The untrained teacher created her own mathematics lessons without a prescribed text. Both teachers had short mini lessons and time for exploration with guided questioning by the teacher. Both teachers were guided by the mathematics benchmarks for kindergarten students in Jefferson County. The teachers did not plan together but often debriefed informally on their students' learning and progress.

The students with the untrained teacher demonstrated more risk taking during their explorations, while the students who were with the trained teacher were hesitant to explore and when they did explore, their explorations were shorter than in the untrained teacher's class. They demonstrated disinterest sooner than the other class. As stated earlier, both classes achieved 90% proficiency or better on the kindergarten mathematics benchmarks. Both teachers indicated they valued participating in the action research and will continue the process in the future.

There have been lessons learned from inquiry conducted at Stillwater over the years. Inquiry or action research can produce a culture of inquiry that nudges professional dialogue about teaching among staff members. The outcomes of inquiry have the potential to affect the immediate classroom practice through deeper analysis of specific events and issues in the classroom. Conducting action research assists teachers to make the connections between educational research and teaching practice. And inquiry can improve student and teacher learning.

The partnership has made cutting-edge program changes to better educate teachers and to better serve the schools in the UCD partnership. The program strives for shared purposes and the participation of many partner voices. We hope conversations of inquiry will continue at Stillwater Elementary School and that human capital will continue to grow through the process.

The Impact of Human Capital

Building human capital is a communitywide opportunity. Each of these essays illustrates how people can make a difference through collaboration, believing that all students can learn, and being prepared to be reflective practitioners who are lifelong learners themselves. External capital can provide the resources and support of a community; internal capital can provide the systems to ensure that processes are in place so that activities happen in an organized and appropriate manner; but it is ultimately the human capital that makes it happen, that portrays the cultural competence, and that is willing to grow and change in the interest of student learning.

Chapter 7

Changing School Culture

It is not unusual to hear principals and site coordinators talk about how the culture in their school has changed as a result of the partnership. Explaining exactly what that means is another story, and a complex one at that. "School culture refers to the sum of the values, cultures, safety practices, and organizational structures within a school that cause it to function and react in particular ways" (McBrien & Brandt, 1997, p. 89). Patterson, Purkey, and Parker (1986) summarize the general knowledge base regarding school culture:

- School culture does affect the behavior and achievement of elementary and secondary school students (though the effect of classroom and student variables remains greater).
- School culture does not fall from the sky; it is created and thus can be manipulated by people within the school.
- School cultures are unique; whatever their commonalities, no two schools will be exactly alike—nor should they be.
- To the extent that it provides a focus and clear purpose for the school, culture becomes the cohesion that bonds the school together as it goes about its mission.
- Though we concentrate on its beneficial nature, culture can be counterproductive and an obstacle to educational success; culture can also be oppressive and discriminatory for various subgroups within the school.
- Lasting fundamental change (e.g., changes in teaching practices or the decision-making structure) requires understanding and, often, altering the school's culture; cultural change is a slow process.
- An examination of school culture is important because, as Goodlad's study (1984) pointed out, "alike as schools may be in many ways, each school has an ambience (or culture) of its own, and

101

further, its ambience may suggest to the careful observer useful approaches to making it a better school" (p. 81).

In the previous chapters, we've seen highlights of various PDSs as they have written about one intangible asset in their partnership. Some of the schools have been professional development schools (PDSs) for 12 years and some for only 9 months. But, what they have in common is the desire to be intentional about their work; they believe that they truly are a PDS and committed to lifelong learning and renewal through the partnership. We believe that if these schools think about building external, internal, and human capital and manage intangible assets they will change the culture of the school.

The last two stories are from schools that have been PDSs for over 10 years. They have documented some of their cultural change in hopes that others can see the potential for developing PDSs. The first is about a comprehensive high school and the second, a middle school, both highly impacted schools with linguistically diverse learners and mixed socio-economic families.

Becoming a Professional Development School

Stan Kyed and Mike Marlow

Norse High School is a school rich in history and tradition. Faculty and staff are committed to all students learning successfully in a safe, nurturing, disciplined and challenging environment. Norse has approximately 2,400 students: 58% Caucasian, 31% Hispanic, 7% Asian, 3% Black. Twenty percent of the students receive free or reduced lunch, and 16% are English as second language learners. Norse has been a professional development school since 1993 and participated in the original development of the National Council for Accreditation of Teacher Educators' PDS standards.

Making day-to-day progress toward the vision requires open communication, hard work, and determination. It also requires continual assessment to inform stakeholders of the progress. Two years ago, a group of high school teachers finished the first day of school, walked down the hall to another classroom, opened their notebooks, and began their master's degrees. Now known to the faculty as "the cohort," they didn't really know each other as they began their school-based master's degree. Said one member of the beginning, "I remember walking in the first day and I didn't know some of those people. I recognized the faces and I knew they were teachers but I didn't know anything about them. I wasn't sure what subject they taught."

Two years later, another member of the cohort, who was among the first 11 to graduate, offered an appraisal of the group's collegiality:

> One of the greatest gifts of these past 2 years has been the opportunity to have meaningful conversations with other teachers about the work we do, about theories and designs of pedagogy, about the issues we face everyday [sic], from political agendas to media scrutiny to what were [sic] going to do about Johnny who falls asleep in our first hour. I see that we have a real need to share, to deliberate, to debate, to discuss.

This master's cohort is just one initiative in a long line of professional development initiatives at Norse High School. Norse High School continually finds new ways to build human capital through its partnership with the university. The results since 1998 have been stunning. The story of how it came to this position is tracked in this essay, and lessons can be learned from Norse's journey to putting the professional development into PDS.

Although Norse High School has been a National Network for Educational Renewal (NNER) PDS with the University of Colorado Denver since 1993, the real movement toward becoming a fully functioning PDS began in 1998 with the first written articulation of the partnership's core values. A series of activities and meetings led to the recognition of a philosophical position that would underpin all partner decision making. These core values at first were only used in partner activities but since have become important considerations in all school decision making. Rather than being immediately identified they coalesced over a period of time and through a series of discussions. In the early stages of the partnership, a thinly veiled uncertainty existed in the relationship between the university and the school. The university faculty was unsure how to properly approach school personnel with university program needs, and the school personnel had concerns about the university's judgment and knowledge of actual school needs and operation. This led to a period of "testing" each other, during which the major philosophical components developed from open discussion over time and directly related to a series of specific activities. The core components, mutual decision making, mutual benefit, and *kuleana* (defined later) were first openly expressed as a base for partner operations during 1998. Written articulations of these core values evolved in an Institute for Educational Inquiry state of the partnership document, in a written preparation for an NNER meeting in Seattle, and an NNER self-portrait.

In the development of the philosophy, our first goal was to overcome separations between the partners. The discussions made clear the importance of the human side of things, not only for colleagues at the university and the PDS, but also in the work with the preservice teachers. This type of relationship between partners contrasts sharply with the traditional "university as ivory tower" approach, where the university enters the school as a superior partner with all the answers. We saw two elements as essential to the development of this degree of collegiality: (a) building strong relationships and (b) validation of colleagues as equals.

Joint Decision Making

Commonly, participants in described partnerships have strikingly different roles within the relationship, with each contributing to the common enterprise particular talents, experiences, and perspectives, which may or may not be valued because of the status of the partner. We determined that minimizing notions of status and maximizing mutual decision making within a partnership contributes to a more effective relationship and recognized each partner's abilities and contributions. This concept was the first developed of the core philosophies. It emerged in a series of meetings where participants were getting to know each other and ground rules were being developed. The discussion began with a perception on the part of the school faculty that the university thought it was entering the school to fix it and not only knew all the school's issues but the best way to rectify them. This of course was not the university's position, nor was it true about the school needing fixing, but it certainly opened up the discussion. Soon the conclusion was reached that all partnership activities would be mutually decided upon and that all concerns could and would be openly expressed and discussed. This concept has continued to the present, helping resolve issues that might cause distrust and result in project failure if kept hidden. As a result, university representatives are commonly present at school meetings, including serving on some faculty hiring teams, and in turn, school faculty serve on teacher education boards and committees at the university. In each case all members carry the same voting power and have equal opportunity to express opinions.

Mutual Benefit

A long-term partnership must be beneficial to each participant in ways that contribute to their day-to-day operation. Time to commit to additional projects that may or may not contribute to one's immediate mission is limited. In a real sense, if one partner is not specifically benefiting from the activity, they may limit the amount of time and effort they are able to contribute and thus impact the quality of the product. To alleviate this issue, partnership activities must be carefully designed to consider mutual needs. One partnership activity, which took place in 1999, demonstrates this premise. The university's Initial Professional Teacher Education program (IPTE) had a need to arrange a large number of classroom observations for the newest teacher candidates in its program. In the secondary teacher candidate cohort, classroom visits were a required experience in one of their first courses. These initial visits did not contribute in any recognized way to the PDS's classroom operation. In addition, the school already had a large number of teacher candidates in the building completing their teaching residencies as interns from earlier cohorts. The resident interns do make valuable contribution to both the classroom operation and the school, so their presence can be construed as beneficial to both partners.

Discussions began on how we might make these first visits beneficial for Norse as well as for the university. Fortunately, Norse had an immediate need, centered on a North Central Association (NCA) accreditation process and National Council for Accreditation of Teacher Education (NCATE) professional development partnership review. Norse had been selected for a pilot study on how to assess school–university teacher education partnerships. Regarding the two reviews, the high school needed to collect large amounts of data on classroom practice, student and teacher attitudes toward education, and impacts of the partnership on its academic mission. A decision was made to join the university's need for a student observation site and the high school's need to collect large amounts of data for its upcoming reviews by developing an intense day of observation covering all aspects of school operation in a way that would be mutually beneficial.

This project brought the new secondary teacher candidates to the school for a full day of data collection. These candidates were responsible for completing data forms and interviews in each of the classes they were assigned to visit. The teacher candidates collected data from a total of 239 class periods during the "Day in the Life" project, using the provided tools. These tools measured the type of management and teaching strategies that teachers used in their classrooms. The collected data was entered by the clinical teachers at the end of the observation day and became immediately available to the PDS for analysis. In turn, the teacher candidates had the opportunity to practice their observation skills and engage in the collection of data. Thus, their entry experience in a PDS served to highlight not only the pedagogical emphasis of their program but also the inquiry perspective the partnership hopes to enable through the building of a public school–university community.

Kuleana

We suggest that maintaining a partnership requires recognition of the complexity of the relationship. Putting the pieces together is certainly not enough; continuous assessment, reflection on the findings, and addressing the changing needs of each partner in a way that results in mutual benefit all contribute to this complexity. The building of trust based on personal relationships is at the heart of this philosophical approach. Trust is necessary for a partnership to be consistently successful over the long term. A major component of trust is the responsibility to learn what is important to others and to act accordingly. The root of this idea originates for us with the Hawaiian term *kuleana*, which generally refers to the concept of "responsibility." For instance, a Hawaiian might say, "My family is my kuleana"; the term suggests a sense of accountability that cannot be denied. We believe that this accountability implies that we recognize what is important to those for whom we are responsible and, as a consequence, feel a strong commitment to support them in realizing their goals. Kuleana, as we use it in our partnerships, is a feeling of caring and a sense of advocacy. It emphasizes the relationship between individuals, not just institutions, and demands consideration of the needs and feelings of all partners. Without this component the partnership rings hollow. Kuleana is the binding glue that solidifies all effective relationships. In developing our partnership activities, the presence of kuleana is at the forefront. During preliminary partnership discussions, the needs of all partners are specifically identified, and throughout subsequent activities we periodically assess whether or not all of those needs continue to be met.

Although kuleana has led to many of the partnership project choices, the individual professional development of the school faculty most represents this philosophical approach. Throughout, individual faculty professional needs have been addressed by the following:

- Individual courses offered and commonly taught in the school by school faculty
- A complete master's cohort program with 9 of the 12 courses taught in the school

- Numerous special-topic workshops
- Copresentation opportunities at national conferences
- Coauthoring of professional journal articles
- Field experience for faculty in content areas
- Utilization of experienced content teachers as experts in university projects
- Division of the school into 11 professional development teams

The following are examples of individual professional growth:

- Sixteen present faculty received their teaching license through the UCD IPTE program.
- Thirty-two present faculty members have received or have nearly completed a master's degree from UCD.
- Five faculty members are presently in the UCD doctoral program.
- Ten faculty members have taught university level courses.
- Four science faculty members developed regional praxis preparation materials and are scheduled to teach the praxis prep workshops.
- Six faculty members are in leadership positions with the UCD Wyoming Science Inquiry Center.
- Eleven faculty members chair school professional development teams.
- Six faculty members serve as in-house instructional coaches (faculty release).

Effective collaboration considers the three components—mutual decision making, mutual benefit and kuleana—in all decision making. It is only through a commitment to the complex interplay between the three that we can maintain a community that is real and meaningful to all participants.

Becoming a Professional Development School

There are many lessons to be learned from analyzing this partnership. We summarize a few of the more important findings:

The major difficulty of working together in a school and university PDS partnership is the difficulty in overcoming the conflicting interests of each partner, on both the institutional and personal level. *Kuleana* implies the responsibility to pay attention to and work for the interests of the other. There must be mutual benefit for partners to ensure continued success. We do not suggest a transactional view, where each act is accompanied by an accounting of benefit; rather, we suggest a view illustrated by the concept of kuleana—the constant assessment of what is important to other players, and action in that regard. In other words, it is the responsibility of the partners to recognize what is important to the other partners in order to lead to a more trusting relationship. This may require a great deal of effort on the part of one partner with no apparent benefit in the short term. A true partnership requires patience and recognition of human need and frailty. However, minimizing the notion of status and maximizing mutual decision-making lead to a more effective relationship.

However, by engaging in cooperative planning and teaching one another what they know about teaching, learning, and leading, the partners have developed a sense of trust. This trust has been further strengthened by the players' demonstration of kuleana, their feelings of responsibility to recognize and support each other's professional needs and concerns. This has led to the initial skepticism that the school felt about the partnership being replaced by a feeling of trust and common purpose between the school and the university. The personalizing of interactions between partners was shown to be a strong reason for the success of this partnership, cultural competence, growth, and change.

Changing the Culture of a School

Jennifer Weese and Bill Munsell

Creek Middle School is a large, suburban middle school situated in what many describe as the largest mobile home community in the country. Located in the northern fringe of the Denver metropolitan area, Creek is a Title I school serving sixth- through eighth-grade students from a culturally, educationally, and economically diverse population. Creek has been a professional development school since 1993.

Prior to joining the professional development school partnership, Creek faculty and staff did an extraordinary job of trying to best meet the needs of their students but frequently struggled with an unfair stigma attached to the school by outsiders as a less-than-desirable assignment. The students were seen as challenging, the climate was perceived as unhealthy, and the self-concept of many of those working diligently to make a difference suffered from the unfair image others had of the school. Further, the social and behavioral needs of the students frequently became distractions from the faculty's desire to focus on their academic needs. Simply put, it was a challenging assignment that by its nature had a dampening impact on the school's image and sense of efficacy. While there was a commitment on the part of many faculty members to grow professionally, the dynamics of the school's environment and absence of an institutionalized program made teachers generally cautious of and apprehensive about adding the challenges of "new" programs.

Before Creek's involvement in the partnership, the culture was described as one in which the teachers simply came to teach. A former principal shared the observation that "there was commitment from part of the faculty to grow professionally, but that commitment was very tenuous. Creek was a difficult school in which to teach."

For the faculty within the university, this was exactly the school setting they were seeking to support. They quickly embraced the challenges of the existing school culture and became an integral part of the long-term professional growth of the school's preservice and existing teachers.

In 1993, as the result of discussions involving the principal of the middle school, university staff, and the principals of neighboring feeder schools, a decision was made to form a school–university partnership as a cluster of teaching, learning, and training schools. Significant changes followed the collaboration within this cluster of schools. The principal at the time of the partnership's inception described the process:

> We joined the partnership and became a cluster of teaching/learning/training schools. We exchanged teacher candidates, hired teacher interns, shared site professors, and worked together in many ways to develop practices that would address the needs of the students within our cluster of schools. The structure and the human and material resources that the partnership added helped this change occur. The site coordinator and site professor were instrumental in supporting, supervising, and training teacher candidates and teacher interns. These people also provided the clinical teachers additional resources, as well as empowering them to be thoughtful and instructive about their teaching practices.

From the outset, the partners committed themselves to Goodlad's (1984) concept of simultaneous educational renewal, as well as to the desire to provide extra adult support focused on meeting the needs of the students. The program at the school successfully engaged clinical teachers, teacher candidates, a faculty site coordinator, and a university site professor with ongoing support from the school, school district, and university administration. Partnership activities over the years included countless internships, action research projects, and building-level professional development. Master teachers served as site coordinators and continue to support the partnership in their pursuit of advanced degrees, national certification, principal licensure, and other expanded leadership roles within the district.

The case can be reasonably made that virtually every experience for a teacher intern, who is a novice to the classroom, can be defined as a professional development experience. On the other hand, the lasting impact of a partnership experience on the practice of clinical teachers at the outset is more difficult to ascertain. As a matter of practice, teachers at Creek are not asked to serve as clinical teachers until they have had at least 3 years of successful experience in their own classroom. While the impact of the extra support in the classrooms and the benefits of the extended internship for teacher candidates were both apparent early in the partnership, the experience requirement for clinical teachers and the need for sufficient implementation time were factors in realizing the full benefit of the partnership to the school.

In an effort to assess the extent to which the partnership has impacted the school, experienced clinical teachers (many of whom were former teacher candidates) and administrators were asked to respond to a number of reflective questions on the extent to which they felt their involvement in the partnership impacted their teaching practice, the culture and climate of Creek, student learning, the preparation of teacher candidates, and the overall value of the program. Their responses were thoughtful and paint an accurate picture of 10 years of successful partnership. Administrators, teachers, parents, students, and interns all communicated by way of their responses to the questions, as well as in their daily discussions, the belief that the involvement of the school in the partnership has had a positive impact on their teaching practice

Concerning the partnership's bearing on individual teaching practices, all of the clinical teachers responded with the belief that the partnership experience had had a positive impact on their teaching practice. However, even more powerful than their feelings of the experience as positive or negative are their personal descriptions of the impact they feel the experience has had on their practice. Their voices speak eloquently of their personal renewal as practicing professionals. One social studies teacher said,

> Having teacher candidates in my room causes me to do the job of teaching "out loud" all day, including lesson planning, discipline,

conversations with students, assessment, and my mistakes. Discussing decisions each day gives me a "second look" at the process I use to make decisions. I also seem to try to be more clear with students on days a teacher candidate is here.

Another teacher commented,

My involvement with the partnership has had a very positive impact on my teaching practice and I feel strongly that it is helping me grow as a teacher. I am much more aware of what I do and why I do what I do, because I share and discuss often what I am doing and/or what the teacher candidate is doing and why. As a clinical teacher, I am exposed to new ideas and new styles of teaching. I am able to ask questions and discuss students' needs and how to best help them learn. I am able to share in the teaching of students and dedicate more time to meeting individual needs. As I grow and learn and get better and better at what I do, my students benefit, as does the teacher candidate, who is both a learner and teacher in this process. In my experience, two teachers in the classroom are definitely better than one, and without a doubt the impact on my teaching practice is a positive one.

Over time, the benefits became obvious, and the participation grew steadily and the staff and student acceptance so natural that the partnership became, and remains, an essential part of the school culture. One teacher summarized the transformation like this:

I believe that the partnership has had a profoundly positive impact on the culture and climate of Creek. Throughout the building, there is a sense of excitement and interest that I believe can be attributed to the presence of the partnership. It is invaluable for student teachers to be able to work with quality professionals in a school setting. It is also extremely beneficial for the children to interact with teacher candidates. The partnership adds a sense of cooperation and community that is an important part of Creek.

Another teacher added,

I think the climate at Creek is nurturing and collaborative. We work together, we are open to new and innovative ideas, we share ideas and resources, and we help each other learn. I think the partnership helps this be an ongoing process.

The impact is evident, the results significant.

The partnership has created an atmosphere of unity and collaboration among staff members and teacher candidates that undoubtedly has affected the quality of the educational environment. Because of its engagement in the partnership, Creek Middle School sees itself as a very different place than before. All the ancillary benefits of the PDS experience, including improved teacher training, extra support for students, site-based professional development, professional dialogue around the practice of teaching, and so forth—the intellectual capital of the school—aside, university partnership resides in the cultural shift that has resulted in how the school community perceives itself. The school and the faculty see themselves as an institution and body of professionals with skills from which others can learn. Instead of the school being associated with its earlier stigma, it is now perceived both internally and externally as a PDS capable of both reflecting on and improving instructional practice as well as instructing others. Perhaps one teacher provided the best summary of the experience:

> I feel the partnership has pushed our staff to examine how we teach and not allowed us to get stagnant. Clinical teachers are forced to be more reflective teachers as they communicate with their teacher candidates. Teacher candidates in turn bring in new methodologies and questions that also help direct teacher and ultimately student learning.

Because of the partnership program, Creek Middle School has changed forever and for the better. As a school that perceives itself as having an intellectual capital that has value for both the professional staff and the students it has embarked on a journey that has resulted in pervasive professional growth and a new image of itself.

Chapter 8

Lessons Learned and Building Intellectual Capital

Carole Basile and Deanna Sands

The complexities of systems and institutions make it very difficult to create change, and just partnering doesn't bring about the changes that we would all hope for. Partnerships are not perfect—maintaining and sustaining activities and relationships as people come and go in both institutions is like starting over. As we maintain records of state test scores for all of our professional development schools (PDSs), it looks like trends in the stock market. As we try to be accountable for student learning, we realize that we cannot control all the variables that enter into the ups and downs in these test scores. We know that we are committed to schools that are working under difficult conditions, and building intellectual capital is difficult under conditions of high-stakes testing, accountability, and funding cuts and in urban school contexts that can be volatile and under a constant barrage of reform strategies.

However, since 1993, the university has learned a lot about what it takes to work with schools and school districts, and schools have learned a lot about what it takes to work with a university. The university has learned that schools and teachers have a lot to teach universities about the everyday life of teachers and their students and families and that all the best theory in the world doesn't always play out in the way one might expect. Because the partnership allows university faculty to spend at least one day a week in schools, faculty are constantly reminded that schools are complex, and the pressures on the people who support them are enormous. The university is also reminded that it is only one constituent to whom districts need to pay attention, and the planning cycles that schools and universities operate from do not always mesh. Faculty in universities can think long-term and broadly, while school personnel are often operating in a short-term, emergency mode especially when

113

new programs are introduced, accountability is ratcheted up, or when students are in crisis.

On the other hand, people who work in schools have learned that universities do not have to be ivory towers and that many education faculty come from school backgrounds and are happiest when they have opportunities to be closer to students. School personnel have also learned that faculty from education, liberal arts, and other schools or colleges can be viable resources. They have begun to understand the difference between student teachers and university supervisors who pop in and those who are in it for the long run. School faculty understand that we share common goals in terms of student achievement at the preschool through postsecondary levels, that funding is a worry for everyone, and that universities are also very complex.

In the end, those who work in both universities and schools begin to recognize the needs of the others' institutional structures and bureaucracies and issues of sustainability. People within each system learn lessons that fall into the intellectual categories that we've used throughout this book. In this chapter, we again use those categories as a framework for thinking about what we've learned about partnerships since 1993, some things we've learned and done better over the years, and some things about which we are still learning and trying to figure out how to make better.

Lessons Learned About Building External Capital

One of the first things we've learned is that the work of PDSs cannot be done solely with individual schools; it must also include work at the school district level. In our case, the school district relationship has become an extension of the work in individual schools. As district personnel change, so does the effort to support, maintain, grow, and fund the PDS model. In different school districts, the work looks different because each one had different purposes in mind when the work started. Administration in one district saw PDSs as a way to recruit new teachers, and yet another saw PDSs as a way to improve student learning in low-achieving schools. In one small school district (nine schools), a decision was made to make every school a PDS by placing teacher candidates in every school. The problem was that, because of the university funding structures, site professors were working across schools and not doing the in-depth professional learning work that could be done when they worked within just one school. So, having more teacher candidates was good, but since site professors and site coordinators did not have time to work together, or when site professors really didn't have a chance to work deeply with clinical teachers, then the value added of the partnership diminished. That model lasted 3 years, and we were back to fewer schools and thinking about how the partnership could impact the other schools even if they didn't have teacher candidates.

In another school district, funding for site coordinators became a concern. We have been very fortunate to have district administrators who have continually advocated for the partnership and "found" money from Title I funds and other sources to continue paying for the additional person. In the meantime, site professors and site coordinators and district and university administrators have been meeting monthly for 2 years to develop new models for PDSs that utilize existing resources and set the course for the PDSs to be a resource for the school district through recruiting, extending induction to an emerging teacher leadership program, and working with other university personnel to begin looking at PDSs for all university partners. This created a gap for districts who had hoped to recruit or retain teacher candidates in new teacher positions.

In a third district, we have now added a high school so that the district would have a full articulation area (elementary, middle school, high school) as PDSs. Faculty within these schools are working together to think about articulation of content and instruction. We believe that this will also help the district keep teacher candidates at the secondary level. In the past, secondary students could do a middle school internship, but when it was time to do a high school internship (teacher candidates need to do both within their 800 hours), they would have to leave the district because a middle school placement was not available.

In every school district, it takes constant communication. We invite district administrators to visit schools and facilitate site professor year-end reviews in PDSs. We also keep in touch with principals and over the years have hosted monthly or quarterly meetings for principals. Since 2004, we have created a partner principal institute that provides professional learning for principals related to their role as principal in a PDS and how to manage knowledge and resources of the partnership.

External capital is also growing knowledge of the partnership within the school walls. Typically, when we bring on a new school, we provide professional learning to clinical teachers about coaching, coteaching, performance-based assessments, and the overall concept of PDSs. In 2004, we brought on another high school and planned a professional learning day. The principal invited every single staff member (including custodians, secretaries, and cafeteria staff) to the event—123 people attended and learned all about the partnership, coaching, and coteaching and how to utilize the resources of the partnership. They don't do anything in the school without asking, "How can the university partnership help us with this?" Now, when we bring on a new school, we make sure everyone is "at the table."

External capital is also built through the external community, parents, businesses, community leaders, nonprofit support agencies, and others. In principal institutes, we have brainstormed lists of the things that principals can do to increase recognition of the school as a PDS within the community. These ideas include creating a list of intangible assets using the intangible asset indicators so you have talking points about the PDS ready when asked, including information about partnership activities in your school newsletter; hosting an open house for the community that "shows off" the partnership (especially funders, parents, realtors, and district administrators); adding the university logo to the school letterhead or simply adding "in partnership with _____ University)"; putting "Professional Development School" on your marquee; advertising partnership events in your local paper; mentioning the partnership at least twice a day; making sure the partnership is mentioned on your Web site and teacher candidate photos are present alongside teachers and staff; and intersecting the partnership with all school activities.

In addition, the university has provided banners for each school and posters that have quotes from clinical teachers, site professors, site coordinators, principals, and teacher candidates. In many PDSs, there is a partnership bulletin board where we showcase pictures, histories, and aspirations of teacher candidates and clinical teachers. We have also created a video and brochure highlighting the benefits of the partnership. We've learned that PDSs have to market who they are and their benefits to students just like any other "specialty" school (e.g., magnet, Montessori, dual language, charter).

Teacher candidates in the program also help build external capital through legacy or service learning projects. The purpose of these projects is for teacher candidates to give back something to the schools that supported their learning during their professional internship experiences. Over the years, teacher candidates have done a myriad of projects—developing level thematic units, building schoolyard habitats or gardens, creating long-term art projects (i.e., hallway murals, garden sculptures, quilts), developing calendars with home activities for parents (Spanish and English), tape-recording books to help nonreaders at home, or hosting parent events. We have learned that the closer the project is to the community, the better it is. Not only does it build external capital, it provides the school with greater communication and outreach to its community at large, in which teachers often do not have time for in their busy days.

Reaching out to the professional community is another important external capital goal. We have continued to understand the importance of the teachers in our PDSs participating in local, regional, and national conferences, attaining their master's degrees, completing principal licensure programs, and in one school, there are five teachers who are completing or have completed their doctoral degrees. Site professors have written numerous publications with teachers and site coordinators about inquiry projects in PDSs, and these have always been important for the community and for the authors.

Paying attention to external capital in recent years has helped us to reach out to a broader constituency, think about how to partner with other partners (i.e., after-school programs, AmeriCorps volunteers, reading and math projects, Boy and Girl Scouts, athletics) at the school, and help the school build bridges with parents and families. The sustainability of partnerships between universities, schools, and school districts depends on how visible we are and the benefits the partnership brings to the whole school community.

Internal Capital

This entire book has been written to ensure that everyone in the partnership thinks intentionally about how to use and manage the knowledge and resources that the partnership brings to a PDS. For that to happen, systems must be in place in schools, school districts, and the university. For example, schools have to have a system for incorporating the site professor in its leadership team and for thinking about how to use technology to help teachers and teacher candidates share information and resources. School districts need systems for recruiting teacher candidates from PDSs for the district early enough to keep them in the district (something that has been very difficult for some of our districts). Principals must understand their administrative role in the partnership by developing systems for distributing leadership, effectively utilizing human capital, and communicating partnership outcomes with parents and community members. Internal capital also includes things like providing office space (even if it is just a corner desk) for the site professor to put things in while in the school, having mailboxes for teacher candidates, inviting the site professor to be part of the leadership team, and making sure everyone is asking how the partnership could be helpful in any situation.

Five years ago, we received grant funding to work with every school's leadership team to get them thinking about how the partnership could benefit them and help increase student learning. We started by looking at school improvement plans for evidence of where the partnership was already included. Not one school had resources from the partnership written into the plan—they were not utilizing the site professors' expertise, thinking about how teacher candidates could cover classrooms while teachers worked with kids who needed the most help, or how to use reduced tuition dollars that the university provides to help teachers gain their master's degrees. This doesn't mean that nothing was actually happening, and we all know that school improvement plans are often written and forgotten, but this told us that there was no intentional conversation going on and things in PDSs just happened. Since then, we haven't stopped talking about intentionality and continue to institutionalize the use of the intellectual capital framework in order to provide clear and concrete ways of looking at what's happening in each school and codifying the systems that have been incorporated to make it happen. Is this occurring in every PDS? No, but at least we're being explicit about it.

The final lesson about internal capital involves university faculty and their need to do research. Many site professors are tenured or tenure-track faculty, and they have figured out ways to incorporate their research agenda into the needs of the school. However, it takes time and internal systems to make sure that the faculty's research not only informs the school but is generalizable to the larger professional academic community as well. Site professors have had to be very intentional as to how to best integrate their teaching, research, and service within the PDS context. In addition, we have found that site professors have worked side by side with principals to develop systems that help both the school and the university understand how to work with each other better and extend conversations about personnel, program issues, and instructional improvement.

Human Capital

The lessons learned about human capital are numerous. The university is always learning about how to work better with teachers, principals, and district administrators; the schools are always discovering new ways to utilize teacher candidates, site professors, and site coordinators. Our lessons learned about building human capital have to do with changing roles and relationships.

First, there is the role of site coordinator, which some would say is the most critical role of the partnership. In the beginning, the site coordinator was only a partnership site coordinator with responsibilities for the partnership related to the four partner functions (professional learning, teacher preparation, inquiry, renewal of curriculum). The district and the university set up a funding model that would allow the school to have two teacher candidates who had just completed their licensure program in place at the beginning of each year to temporarily replace the teacher leader who became the site coordinator. It was a complicated funding structure, but for a time it worked. As funding became tighter and schools could no longer afford to have "temporary teachers" (although many of them became permanent), the roles of the site coordinators changed. Now, different districts do different things to create the role of site coordinator: some still use the old model of using two new teachers for one master teacher; others use building-level instructional, math, or literacy coaches in a dual role; other schools are utilizing part-time "retired but not tired" teachers or administrators; and some are using assistant principals or other teachers in the building to fulfill the role. Every school understands the importance of the role of the site coordinator and how they liaison with the university, and every school is attempting to keep the model in place, but it is becoming very difficult in times of funding and budget cuts.

Another lesson learned in schools is to take advantage of the life experiences of teacher candidates and to integrate their skills to support students. The average age of our students is about 28 or 29 years, and many are second-career students who are former engineers or accountants or come from other professional careers. They have traveled extensively and bring to the classroom a wealth of applied knowledge and practice that can further students' understanding of how topics connect to the world. Schools have also figured out how to begin thinking about utilization of teacher candidates in classrooms so that professional learning can take place with teachers in buildings. A couple of the earlier essays refer to the ability of building personnel to offer professional learning opportunities that formerly couldn't be offered because of teacher contracts and the inability to pay or lack of substitutes. Schools have also learned that with teacher candidates in the classroom, clinical teachers can work with the students who need the most help instead of farming them out to tutors or paraprofessionals.

University and school faculty share in the decision making related to teacher candidate admissions and placements. They learned that giving prospective students too many choices about placements didn't work because they would usually choose to go to a school that looked like the school where they went as a child. Faculty are learning how to place teacher candidates in contexts that challenge their core beliefs and experiences with respect to diversity. We still have teacher candidates (or husbands or parents) who call after they receive their placement and ask for a transfer because they are afraid to work in a particular neighborhood. We also have teacher candidates (and faculty) who find it difficult to have tough conversations about race, equity, privilege, disproportionality, and cultural differences. We are paying more attention to these issues in courses and in internships so that we can build human capital and increase cultural competence in all partner participants.

Inquiry is also a dimension of building human capital, and it's one of the functions of the partnership. Prior to 2000, every teacher candidate was required to take an action research course, and as a result, each teacher candidate developed an action research project within his or her PDS. Because teacher candidates engaged in action research, we saw inquiry take on more prominence among our clinical teachers as well. In 2000, the state of Colorado mandated teacher education standards that did not include inquiry and significantly limited the total number of credit hours that could be required by programs, and so we were forced to take the action research course out of the licensure curriculum. It was a great loss for our PDSs, and we find that less attention to inquiry has resulted.

As mentioned earlier, there are many lessons learned in the area of human capital. We've learned more about coaching everyone, not just teacher candidates, and how to do it simultaneously. We've learned that coteaching is a must, but we need to be explicit with clinical teachers and teacher candidates if we want it to happen. We know that having a council with all partners at the table for professional learning, policy discussion, and development of assessment and curriculum is a must. Overall, we recognize that without the constant development of human capital the partnership would be stagnant and would probably not be sustainable.

Growth and Change

Professional development schools were created with simultaneous renewal in mind. In other words, there is constant and continuous renewal of both the schools and the university at the same time. Throughout this book, there are a number of examples of simultaneous renewal through professional learning, such as the use of technology to create online community of learners, data-driven assessments completed by teacher candidates that informed the school, university assignments as a school's common assessments, site professors working with K–12 students that created change in their university courses, and redesign of university assignments based on the feedback of teachers and administrators, grants, projects, and research that impacted both schools and the university. The list goes on and on.

Today, PDSs are different for every university and school district that embarks on the model because they all have their own financial and bureaucratic constraints. We know that our model isn't perfect and it doesn't fit everyone, but we believe that we are adding value to the schools and the university every day. We also believe that we have to be intentional about resources and we have to manage knowledge so that we build external, internal, and human capital. As the illustration in Chapter 1 implies, it is then and only then that we can increase cultural competence, promote growth and change in schools and the university, and ultimately impact student learning.

Glossary

clinical teachers. Teachers in partner schools who work directly with *teacher candidates* in school internships.

Initial Professional Teacher Education (IPTE). The name of the University of Colorado Denver program that prepares new teachers for elementary and secondary (English, foreign languages, math, science, social studies, special education) schools.

internships. There are four school internships in the program that are required to total 800 hours in schools.

IPTE Council. Site coordinators and *site professors* who collaboratively make decisions about the program.

National Network for Educational Renewal (NNER). Founded by John Goodlad, NNER's main goal is the simultaneous and interdependent renewal of schools of education, liberal arts colleges, and K–12 schools. The Colorado Partnership for Educational Renewal is one of eleven national sites (and one of two consortiums) with membership in NNER.

leadership teams. A team at each partner school, including the *site professor* and *site coordinator*, that leads the implementation of the partner school functions.

partner principals. A group of all the *professional development school (partner school)* principals and School of Education and Human Development administrators who meet monthly to discuss issues related to work in partner schools.

performance-based assessments. The tools that are used in the program to determine Teacher Candidates' proficiency in the Colorado teacher education standards.

professional development schools (partner schools). Public K–12 schools that work with University of Colorado Denver in fulfilling four functions: new teacher preparation, professional development, research or inquiry, and the renewal of curriculum and instruction in the university and the public schools.

site coordinator. A master teacher who is released from direct responsibility of teaching students to ensure implementation of the *partner school* functions.

site professor. University faculty from the University of Colorado Denver's School of Education and Human Development who work in *partner schools* one day each week to fulfill the four *partner school* functions.

teacher candidates. Students enrolled in University of Colorado Denver *Initial Professional Teacher Education* program prior to licensure.

References

Abdul-Haaq, I. (1998). *Professional development schools: Weighing the evidence*. Thousand Oaks, CA: Corwin Press.

Borko, H., Wolf, S. A., Simone, G., & Uchiyama, K. P. (2003). Comprehensive school reform in culturally and linguistically diverse contexts. *Educational Evaluation and Policy Analysis, 25*(2), 171–201.

Cobb, P., McClain, K. (2006). The collective mediation of a high-stakes accountability program: Communities and networks of practice. *Mind, Culture, and Activity, 13*(2), 80–100.

Coburn, C. (2006). Framing the problem of reading instruction: Using frame analysis to uncover the microprocesses of policy implementation. *American Educational Research Journal, 43*(3), 343–379.

Cole, M. (1996) *Cultural psychology: A once and future discipline*. Cambridge, MA: Belknap.

Cole, M. (1999) Cultural psychology: Some general principles and a concrete example. In Y. Engeström, R. Miettinen, R. Punamäki (Eds.), *Perspectives on activity theory* (pp. 87–106). Cambridge, UK: Cambridge University Press.

Cotton, K. (2003). *Principals and student achievement: What the research says*. Alexandria, VA: Association for Supervision and Curriculum Development.

Duffy, G. G. (2003). *Explaining reading: A resource for teaching concepts, skills, and strategies*. New York: Guilford.

Dweck, C. (2002). Messages that motivate: How praise molds students' beliefs, motivation, and performance (in surprising ways). In J. Aronson (Ed.), *Improving academic achievement: Impact of psychological factors on education* (pp. 38–58). New York: Academic Press.

Gill, B., & Hove, A. (1999). *The Benedum collaborative model of teacher education: A preliminary evaluation* (Report prepared for the Benedum Center for Education Reform DB-303-EDU): Rand Education.

123

Goodlad, J. (1984). *A place called school: Prospects for the future*. New York: McGraw-Hill.

Grossman, P., Wineburg, S., & Woolworth, S. (2001). Toward a theory of teacher community. *Teachers College Record, 103*(6), 942–1012.

Heifetz, R. A. (1995). *Leadership without easy answers*. Cambridge, MA: Belknap.

Houston, W. R. (1999). Effects of collaboration on urban teacher education programs and professional development schools. In D. Byrd & J. McIntyre (Eds.), *Research on professional development schools. Teacher education yearbook VII* (pp. 6–28). Thousand Oaks, CA: Corwin.

Hussi, T. (2004). Reconfiguring knowledge management: Combining intellectual capital, intangible assets and knowledge creation. *Journal of Knowledge Management, 8*(2), 36–52.

Kaplan, R., & Norton, D. (1996). *The balanced score card*. Boston, MA: HBS Press.

Killion, J. (2002). *Assessing impact: Evaluating staff development*. Oxford, OH: National Staff Development Council.

Lave, J., Wenger, E. (1991). *Situated learning: Legitimate peripheral participation*. New York: Cambridge University Press.

Leithwood, K. (2004). *Educational leadership: A review of the research*. Philadelphia: Temple University Center for Research in Human Development and Education Laboratory of Student Success.

Marzano, R., McNulty, B., & Waters, T. (2005). *School leadership that works: From research to results*. Aurora, CO: McREL.

McBrien, J., & Brandt, R. (1997). *The language of learning: A guide to education terms*. Alexandria, VA: Association for Supervision and Curriculum Development.

Murrell, P. (1998). *Like stone soup: The role of the professional development school in the renewal or urban schools*. Washington DC: American Association of Colleges of Teacher Education.

National Council for the Accreditation of Teacher Educators. (2003). *PDS outcomes research: Summary of findings of selected studies*. Retrieved January, 25, 2003, from http://www.ncate.org/pds/resources/outcomes.htm

Neubert, G. A., & Binko, J. B. (1998). Professional development schools: The proof is in performance. *Educational Leadership, 55*(5), 44–46.

Newmann, F., & Wehlage, G. (1995). *Successful school restructuring: A report to the public and educators*. Madison, WI: University of Wisconsin Education Center.

No Child Left Behind Act of 2001, Pub. L. No. 107–110, § 115 Stat. 1425 (2002).

Nocon, H., Nilsson, M., & Cole, M. (2004). Spiders, firesouls, and little fingers: Necessary magic in university-community collaboration. *Anthropology and Education Quarterly, 35*(3), 368–385.

Nystrand, M., Wu, L., Gamoran, A., Zeiser, S., & Long, D. (2003). Questions in time: Investigating the structure and dynamics of unfolding classroom discourse. *Discourse Processes, 35*(2), 135–196.

Osguthorpe, R., Harris, R., Harris, M., & Black, S. (Eds.) (1995). *Partner schools: Centers for educational renewal.* San Francisco: Jossey-Bass.

Patterson, J. L., Purkey, S. C., & Parker, J. V. (1986). *Productive school systems for a nonrational world.* Alexandria, VA: Association for Supervision and Curriculum Development.

Pine, G. (2000, April). *Making a difference: A professional development school's impact on student learning.* Paper presented at the AERA Annual Meeting, New Orleans.

Roos, G., & Roos, J. (1997). Measuring your company's intellectual performance. *Long Range Planning, 30*(3), 413–426.

Schmoker, M. (2004). Tipping point: From feckless reform to substantive instructional improvement. *Phi Delta Kappan, 85*(6), 424–432.

Shroyer, G., Wright, E., & Ramey-Gassert, L. (1996). An innovative model for collaborative reform in elementary school science teaching. *Journal of Science Teacher Education, 7*(3), 151–168.

Silns, H., & Mulford, B. (2002). Leadership and school results. In K. A. Leithwood & P. Hallinger (Eds.), *Second international handbook of educational leadership and administration* (pp. 561–612). Dordrecht: Kluwer Academic Publishers.

Sparks, D., & Hirsh, S. (1997). *A new vision for staff development.* Alexandria, VA: Association for Supervision and Curriculum Development.

Stewart, T. A. (1999). *Intellectual capital.* New York, NY: Currency.

Sveiby, K. E. (2001). *Intellectual capital and knowledge management.* Retrieved December 23, 2003, from http://www.sveiby.com/articles/IntellectualCapital

Teitel, L. (2000). *Assessment: Assessing the impacts of professional development schools.* Washington, DC: American Association of Colleges of Teacher Education.

Teitel, L. (2003). *The professional development schools handbook: Starting, sustaining, and assessing partnerships that improve student learning.* Thousand Oaks, CA: Corwin.

Contributors

John Ackelson

John Ackelson, currently retired, was the chief information officer for Adams 12 Five-Star School District in Colorado for over 27 years. He was the chief information officer in the Jefferson County School District in Colorado for over 2 years. John assisted the State Department of Education and various legislative committees in the development of technology planning for school districts as well as the acquisition of funding for the purchase of technology. John assisted the University of Colorado Denver in addressing technology issues in the classrooms of the university and in the classrooms of public K–12 schools.

Heidi Bulmahn Barker

Heidi Bulmahn Barker received her PhD in curriculum and instruction from the University of Illinois at Urbana-Champaign. Prior to her appointment at Regis University, Dr. Barker taught in the teacher education program at University of Colorado Denver. She taught courses in general and special education and worked in professional development schools in the Jefferson County School District. At Regis University, she teaches courses in the special education minor, teaches methods courses for elementary licensure, and supervises preservice teachers in school settings. Dr. Barker's research interests are the personal aspects of school change, preservice and in-service teacher development, relationships between and among teachers and children, and content in the context of school reform.

Carole Basile

Carole G. Basile, associate professor, is a former associate dean of teacher education and director of the Initial Professional Teacher Education program. Her research efforts include papers and presentations related to teacher education, professional development schools, teacher leadership, and interdisciplinary learning. Former director and founder of the Center for Applied Science and Mathematics for Innovation and Competitiveness (CASMIC) at the University of Colorado Denver. She has served as co-principle investigator for NSF-funded math and science partnership and graduate-K12 projects. She has worked on national teacher education and professional development school initiatives with the National Council for the Accreditation of Teacher Education, the National Network for Educational Renewal, and the National Council for Teaching and America's Future.

Betty C. deBaca

Betty C. deBaca is presently the project manager for childcare at the Denver Department of Human Services. She has been in education for 25 years both as a teacher and an elementary school principal. In her tenure with three public school districts in the Denver metro area, she has been instrumental in changes that have positively impacted families and children. These changes have positively impacted the academic achievement of historically underrepresented children. Her work at the local, state, and national level has brought about a new awareness of the importance of the engagement of parents and the community in the education of students.

Susan Field

Susan Field is currently the principal of Woodmen-Roberts Elementary School, an International Baccalaureate Primary Years Program, in Academy School District 20 in Colorado Springs, Colorado. Field has 19 years of experience in public education as a classroom teacher, reading specialist, assistant principal, curriculum coordinator, and principal. She was a professional development school principal for 5 years with the University of Colorado Colorado Springs. Her dissertation research was titled "Research-Based Leadership Practices of the Professional Development School Principal" presented in the spring of 2008.

Cindy Gutierrez

Cindy Gutierrez is the director of teacher education at the University of Colorado Denver. Her research includes work in teacher education, professional development schools, and teacher leadership. Prior to her current role, she was a professional development school site professor and an elementary school teacher.

Beth Hays

Beth Hays retired from the public school system in 2000 after 30 years of classroom and administrative experience. During her administrative experience, she was responsible for teacher evaluation and coaching; staff development; scheduling and data management systems; curriculum development; hiring of staff members; acting as activities director, special education administrator, conflict mediator between parents, student, and teachers; and working with teachers on classroom management and instructional strategies. As a teacher, she was department chairperson, mentor for new staff members, member of school accountability and shared decision-making committees, cheer/pom sponsor, National Honor Society sponsor, and advisor to state and district officers of several student leadership organizations. Her passion has always been to work with students and staff members to achieve the excellence she believes is present in each person.

Oscar Joseph III

Oscar Joseph III is currently principal at Amandla Charter Academy and former associate vice president for branch campus development and academic affairs at the Community College of Denver. He was assistant director of CU-Succeed pre-collegiate programs and assistant professor in the School of Education's Initial Professional Teacher Education/Curriculum and Instruction Division at the University of Colorado Denver. His teaching and expertise includes urban education curriculum design K–16, philosophy and education, ethics and law in education, and social studies methodology.

Denise Kale (deceased)

Denise Kale's career in Adams 12 Five-Star School District in Northglenn, Colorado, spanned the roles of special education teacher, student achievement coach, assistant principal, and site coordinator. Her expertise in mentoring, coaching, and teaching were widely sought after by faculty in urban, inclusive schools. Kale spearheaded a wide array of innovative projects aimed at teaching students to monitor their own behavior and advocate for their needs. Her passion for bringing meaningful initiatives to public schools is evident throughout the university–school district partnership.

Stan Kyed

Stan Kyed is currently dean of students at Mountain Range High School. Prior to this appointment, he was a site coordinator at Northglenn High School, an adjunct faculty member at the University of Colorado Denver, and a high school social studies teacher.

Mike Marlow

Dr. Mike Marlow is a science educator at the University of Colorado Denver in the School of Education and Human Development. His research interests include professional development aspects of teacher education, student research in the science classroom, and building science partnerships. He believes in active learning, which allows the learner to construct a meaningful understanding of the information being presented through experiences such as educational travel and field studies, presentations at national conferences, and internships at science institutions and labs.

Christine McConnell

Christine McConnell is a family and consumer science teacher at Arvada West High School. She has had the opportunity to focus her work on encouraging the best and brightest to consider teaching as a career path. McConnell is a state trainer for the Teacher Cadet Program in Colorado, where she provides comprehensive curriculum training and professional development for the program. In addition to the Teacher Cadet Program, Christine has also served as the first site coordinator of the professional development school at Arvada West High School. In her free time, she enjoys spending time with her family and traveling.

Mike McGuffee

Michael McGuffee is the author and editor of nearly 100 picture books for young readers. He is also the coauthor of *Real ePublishing, Really Publishing* (Heinemann, 2001), which walks teachers through the process of creating, producing, and distributing digital picture books called RealeBooks. McGuffee has devoted the past 10 years creating access to literacy for underserved families across Native American reservations in the Southwest.

Marilyn McIntyre

Wyoming native Marilyn McIntyre is an Initial Professional Teacher Education program site professor in northern metropolitan Denver schools. Before joining University of Colorado Denver in 2002, she worked with preservice teachers at University of Colorado Boulder. She began her teaching career in Clark County, Nevada, where she worked with Teacher Corps, a federal program partnering Clark County and the University of Nevada–Las Vegas. She moved to Colorado in the mid-1970s to join an Individually Guided Education (IGE) program school in the Adams 12 Five-Star School District. She remained in that district until 1999, serving as a classroom teacher, gifted education resource teacher, district-level math and science curriculum specialist, professional development trainer, and assistant principal.

Bill Munsell

The former coordinator of accreditation and school improvement for Adams 12 Five-Star School District in Colorado, Bill Munsell is a current and long-standing site professor and instructor affiliated with the University of Colorado Denver Initial Professional Teacher Education program. His background includes being a secondary science teacher, middle school principal, and former director of the Colorado North Central Association Commission on Accreditation and School Improvement. He has served, and continues to serve, as an experienced team chair and facilitator for numerous domestic and international school accreditation reviews. He was awarded his PhD in 1984 by the University of Colorado Boulder in secondary curriculum, administration, and supervision with a specialization in middle school education. He currently resides in the Denver and Phoenix areas.

Honorine Nocon

Honorine Nocon has a PhD in communication from the University of California–San Diego and is an associate professor of linguistically diverse education at the School of Education and Human Development, University of Colorado Denver. Codirector of the Urban Schools Doctoral Research Lab and a member of the Linguistically Diverse Education's partnership in training teachers in the Denver public schools to work with learners of English as a second language. Nocon teaches in the doctoral program, the master's program, and teacher education. For teacher education, she was a site professor with Denver Public Schools for 4 years. Nocon teaches courses in inclusive practices of education, as well as language and culture and human development.

Flo Olson

During the writing of this book, Florence J. Olson was site coordinator at Jefferson County Open School, Lakewood, Colorado, one of the professional development schools associated with the University of Colorado Denver. She has also been an elementary teacher and an instructional coach for Jefferson County School District. She currently supervises student teachers for Regis University.

Kathy Prior

Kathy Prior has been a Colorado educator for more than 20 years. She has been a classroom teacher, math specialist, staff developer, and mentor teacher. Kathy loves to share her passion of teaching with teacher candidates and new teachers.

Linda Rickert

Linda Rickard is retired from Jefferson County School District, Colorado. She was an outstanding second-grade teacher and later a site coordinator for Semper Elementary School. Rickard initiated the partnership when Semper Elementary was in the planning stages and facilitated a strong relationship between the school and the university.

Deanna Sands

Dr. Deanna Iceman Sands is a professor and the associate dean of research and leadership education in the School of Education and Human Development at the University of Colorado Denver. She coordinates the PhD program in Educational Leadership and Innovation (EDLI) and serves as an advisor and one of the lead faculty for the Urban Schools Doctoral Research Lab. Her research agenda combines issues of quality of life, self-determination, curriculum, assessment, and advocacy for students with and without disabilities. She served as a site professor in Adams County School District 14 in conjunction with her teaching and service to the Initial Professional Teacher Education program, with an emphasis on dual licensure in general and special education.

John Simmons

During his 30 years as a professional educator, John Simmons has taught at every level from early childhood to graduate school. After two decades as a building administrator, now he is serving as an instructional superintendent with Denver Public Schools.

Donna Sobel

Dr. Donna Sobel is currently on the faculty in the Initial Professional Teacher Education program at the University of Colorado Denver. She has served as a site professor at one of University of Colorado Denver's professional development schools for the past 11 years, during which time she has been instrumental in implementing numerous reform initiatives that have resulted in special education curriculum and pedagogy being taught across the general education teacher training program. Sobel's concerns about the attitudes that teachers hold regarding issues of responsive teaching practices have led to a series of investigations of teachers' beliefs about addressing the educational needs of learners from diverse backgrounds and with diverse needs.

Jane Tarkington

Upon retirement from Aurora Public Schools, Jane Tarkington served as a University of Colorado Denver site coordinator at Montview Elementary School from 2001–2007. As an elementary school teacher in California and Colorado since 1967, she taught in self-contained classrooms and in team teaching, nongraded, bilingual/bicultural, and year-round settings. Other career experiences include mentoring new teachers, literacy coaching, and design, development, implementation, and evaluation of curriculum.

Sherry Taylor

Dr. Sheryl V. Taylor is an associate professor at the University of Colorado Denver in the Literacy, Language, and Culturally Responsive Teaching Program in the School of Education and Human Development, where she teaches language acquisition and literacy development, multicultural education, and bilingual education/ESL. She regularly coaches professional teachers in Denver area schools to support English language learners in general education classrooms. Her research examines teachers' cognition and practices in addressing the needs of students from diverse backgrounds and abilities.

Lee Teitel

Lee Teitel has been a researcher, writer, consultant, speaker, and professional development school advocate since 1989. His work focuses on professional development school start-up, sustainability, and impact assessment issues; new leadership roles in professional development schools for teachers and principals; and the development and implementation of national standards for professional development schools. He has led workshops and presentations at the American Association of Colleges for Teacher Education and the American Association for Educational Research and has written numerous articles and monographs on these topics, including two professional development school literature reviews and a handbook for the National Council for the Accreditation of Teacher Education PDS Standards Project and booklets on governance and documenting professional development school impacts for the American Association of College Teacher Educators. He is the author of *The Professional Development Schools Handbook: Starting, Sustaining, and Assessing Partnerships that Improve Student Learning* (Corwin, 2003).

Pat Toomey

Pat Toomey is a student achievement coach at Meridian Elementary School. She is a former site coordinator.

Stephanie Townsend

Stephanie Townsend is a clinical professor at the University of Colorado Denver and the elementary literacy lead instructor in the Initial Professional Teacher Education program. She directed University of Colorado Denver's action research conference for 7 years. Dr. Townsend is currently also a site professor at Edison Elementary School in Denver Public Schools. Her research and teaching foci are elementary literacy assessment and instruction and teacher education.

Maria Uribe

Maria Uribe is principal at an urban school in Denver. She also works as an adjunctive professor at the University of Colorado Denver. She began her teaching career in her native country of Colombia, South America, where she taught for 13 years in bilingual schools. After moving to Denver, Uribe taught first grade for 9 years, she was a coach and the site coordinator for the University of Colorado Denver for 7 years, and for the past year she has been an assistant principal. She has received various recognitions, including the Colorado Association for Bilingual Education president award in 2007. She has published a number of articles on bilingual education and second-language learners. Uribe designed the bilingual program at her elementary school and has presented workshops about literacy strategies for English language learners. Maria earned a masters degree in multicultural and bilingual education from the University of Colorado Boulder and a PhD in educational leadership and innovation from the University of Colorado Denver.

Rick VanDeWeghe

Rick VanDeWeghe is an associate professor of English at the University of Colorado Denver. He was site director for the Initial Professional Teacher Education program at Rishel Middle School, Denver. He is also the director of the Denver Writing Project and field director for the National Writing Project.

Kelli Varney

Kelli Varney is the former site coordinator at Rishel Middle School in Denver. She and Rick VanDeWeghe worked together to develop and implement the study group there that is now a foundational professional development component of the school. Varney currently works as an assistant principal at another Denver Public Schools elementary school.

Jennifer Weese

Jennifer Weese, EdS, is the principal at Meridian Elementary School in the Adams 12 Five-Star School District. She began her teaching career at Niver Creek Middle School in 1988 teaching seventh and eighth grade science and physical education. In 2001, she accepted a position as site coordinator at Niver Creek in partnership with the University of Colorado Denver's Initial Professional Teacher Education program. After 4 years mentoring and supervising teacher candidates, she transitioned to administration in the Adams 12 Five-Star School District. In the 2005–2006 school year, she served as assistant principal at Meridian Elementary and Skyview Elementary. The following year, she served as the interim principal at Meridian and acquired the permanent position in March of 2007. Weese remains active in the Initial Professional Teacher Education program as a lecturer, teaching a section of the undergraduate and graduate course, "Democratic Schooling: Issues of Law and Ethics."

Caron A. Westland

Dr. Caron A. Westland is currently working as a site professor in an elementary professional development school in Jefferson County School District. As a full-time faculty member, she teaches both general and special education courses in the teacher preparation program at the University of Colorado Denver. Additionally, she serves as a faculty advisor for the Student Council for Exceptional Children, building a collaborative relationship with Metropolitan State College of Denver and University of Colorado Denver students and guiding them to become teacher-leaders as they advocate for students with special needs. Her research interests include narrative inquiry, at-risk youth, parental involvement, and the use of the reflective process to connect students with their learning.

Phillip A. White

Phillip A. White, PhD, has taught in elementary schools for 30 years, from kindergarten to sixth grade. At present he is an adjunct faculty member at the School of Education and Human Development, University of Colorado Denver, in the Initial Professional Teacher Education program.

Index